ONE OF
EVERYTHING

ONE OF EVERYTHING

DONNA CAROL VOSS

VANTAGES
BOOKS

VANTAGES BOOKS, LLC
Kaysville, UT 84037

Publisher's Note
As this is a memoir, all incidents recounted herein are true; however, to protect the privacy of some individuals, certain names and details have been changed.

Library of Congress Cataloging-in-Publication Data
Control Number: 2014921248

ISBN 978-0-9906226-0-4

Designed by Gwyn Kennedy Snider
Author photo by Richard Busath
Manufactured in the United States of America

www.vantagesbooks.com

For Cary, the only man I could ever
see myself with in the eternities

"You only live once, but if you do it right, once is enough."
—MAE WEST

INTRODUCTION

"It is better to be hated for what you are
than to be loved for what you are not."
—ANDRÉ GIDE
Autumn Leaves

I am a woman with a past. I never met a door I didn't open. Like Eve in the Garden of Eden, I bet it all on first-hand experience. The only question now is what to tell the broad-shouldered man across from me. He is not right for me—too old, too already-done-that—and I am, improbably now at thirty-eight, determined to start a family. We don't add up on paper, yet his vivid sky blues, leveled at me patiently, waiting for me to speak, pull me in. Soft warmth suffuses through me and despite myself, I see a future. Telling him is only right.

A forgettable sports bar with a summertime Formula One race blaring from each television is the crossroads of my past life and unlikely future. We are alone in the restaurant but for the beer drinkers and occasional margarita skirts lapping the bar. Above our table, a solitary fixture beams its spotlight onto our unfolding passion play, and I hear my cue.

"I need to tell you some things about my history," I start and then hesitate as self-protection battles honest disclosure; I am no stranger to rejection.

"Okay."

He doesn't react visibly, but I know these church boys, so sheltered, so naïve. I'm afraid he will never see me the same way again. My insides, a moment ago so soft and warm, twist into a sinking, dull heaviness. I am no stranger to panic either. At least that's what I would have called it at fourteen had I been able to feel anything after the bomb went off in my life.

My face shows none of the apprehension welling up in my chest. I know this because my gift from the trauma, the silver lining that embroiders its bittersweet edge around every wound, is the ability to project a strength and a confidence so absolute they reveal nothing else. If what doesn't kill you makes you stronger, what almost kills you makes you near invincible. Pretending for years afterward, even to myself, that everything was fine, that I was fine, had solidified into a facade of smoothest granite. Under our bright spotlight, all he sees is a very put-together brunette, a woman who's quite sure of herself and her place in the world. He is, paradoxically, both correct and beguiled.

We met at church, which makes it even more difficult to say the things I have to say. Late to the party of organized religion, I am not haloed in the blushing aura of goodliness he may expect. My crown, rather, is one of hard-fought life experience woven with Siamese twin strands of gratitude and remorse. Every awful, disturbing, exhilarating moment made me who I am, including the ones for which I will have eternal sorrow.

I want to tell him that I ache for many of the things I've done but harbor secret glee for others, certain scandalously thrilling experiences that happen only on the edges of propriety. I need him to understand that some things were done out of emotional pain or the scraggly search for meaning, and some were done out of the darkness of ignorance, but many were done because I hungered for and don't regret the experience. I need him to see that I am not the person I used to be, and yet I vaulted each wave with the same courage and integrity I possess now.

I find his eyes, and he is still there, still patiently waiting. It is now or never.

"I've been divorced," I say, testing the water with my easy one.

He breaks into a broad grin, so handsome with his salt-and-pepper hair.

"Don't feel like the lone ranger on that!" he chuckles somewhat ruefully.

"You as well?" I ask, and he assents his membership in the middle-aged dating club.

"Yep."

I close my eyes and dive all the way under.

"I've also been with lots of men . . . and women . . . I've done illegal drugs and had problems with alcohol . . . I cut myself when I was in college."

Exposing the Xs on my wrist, I extend my arm into the space between us. He glances at the faded white lines before coming back to my face.

The next one, the only one for which I am truly ashamed, is the hardest.

"I committed adultery," I offer quietly. "Not when I was married, but . . . it was still adultery."

I own my past, have repented for much of it, but can undo nothing. Unwaveringly he studies me as I finish my tour de force.

"I had an abortion . . . I worshipped the Goddess and did tarot-card readings every day for ten years . . . I toyed with witchcraft."

My voice has returned to its clear, steady role of carrying forth the cue for his next line in our drama. I have given my best effort, and my apprehension drains away. It is what it is. Either we go forward or we don't.

ONE

"All parents damage their children. It cannot be helped.
Youth, like pristine glass, absorbs the prints of its handlers.
Some parents smudge, others crack, a few shatter childhoods
completely into jagged little pieces, beyond repair."

—MITCH ALBOM

The Five People You Meet in Heaven

What we seek in life rises with us from the crucible of childhood. Early experiences etch themselves like fingerprints, sometimes not so delicately, on our soul. Throughout our life, for good or for ill, they call to other people and conditions. It is not without effort that we interrupt their effect.

At thirteen I already know this.

Perhaps it is my mother who taught me: a vivacious, intelligent woman with negligible awareness of her own fingerprints and a "do as I say, not as I do" approach to parenting. She tells me that her first husband was charismatic like her Irish father, but her second husband, my father, was a man she knew would never hurt her, gentle like her mother. What she doesn't understand, or doesn't want to see, is how her etchings, in turn, etch me and my sister. I see what she doesn't.

My mother knows that we are safe from the alcoholic rages she endured as a child, shaking under her bed until her father had spent himself. Their shadowy echoes in her quiet but steady drinking are easy to miss. Only her artful substitution of yellow coffee mug for whiskey shot glass suggests the nature of her dependence. The acrid stench gives her away, and so, too, does her cut-glass decanter of Ernest and Julio Gallo shimmering in the cold white light of the garage refrigerator, next to the open can of dog food.

"Don't upset Daddy" ruled my mother's childhood home; they lived in fear of his drinking. Our version is "Don't upset Mommy"; we live in fear of a nervous breakdown. My mother has had two, the last one shattering enough for three inpatient weeks of electroshock therapy. She came home, but she never came back.

"Lighten up," she chafes, wanting me to be the happy, silly girl that distracts her from herself.

Instead I am the intense, unsmiling sort who reflects her sadness, the pain she has been unwilling to face and that triggers her brusqueness toward me. I see this, too. Part inherent gift and part survival instinct, I understand her better than she understands me.

My mother dislikes not me but the part of herself she sees in me, a truth that would set me free but for the imprint of her early rejection, the knot of fear squeezed down deep inside me that she is right; I am unlikeable. My own most enduring fingerprint is thereby etched in polarized grooves of supreme self-confidence and inescapable self-doubt. One will carry me through everything about to happen while the other will eat at my core, whispering that smiling faces tell lies, that I am alone.

Steady in the background is my father: tall, dark, and handsome, a virtual teetotaler, whose pattern complements my mother's like perfectly hewn puzzle pieces. His deaf mother, taciturn father, and much older sister, gone by the time he was three, etched the fingerprints that match my mother's lack of intimacy. He rarely speaks. I have never heard him use her first name, and I never see them touch.

Together they create a home that is admirably disciplined and thoroughly middle class: weekly church attendance, piano lessons, exchange students from Europe, and expectations of college. It is devoid of warmth, conversation, and physical affection; a polite, cultured, two-and-a-half-dimensional world.

It is no surprise that I turn elsewhere.

Behavior is as much opportunity as motive, and both for me until now have been weak. Like all children, I think my family standard issue, completely normative parents who laugh together once a year, over half a dozen years, in half a dozen pine-tree-scented campgrounds, over half a dozen family vacations. Notorious optimists, children find the pony in any pile of metaphorical manure; they cling past all reasonable hope that parental attention is coming. Both the realization that it isn't and the arrival of new options tend to show up as a set.

Independent by nature, I am nonetheless designed like all humans for connection, a tiny green shoot struggling up through the thinnest crack of rock toward the sun. I am about to find it, glorious in its heat and life-giving properties, terrible in its ability to shrivel and burn.

Her name is Libby. I don't even like her at first.

I can't afford to like Libby. In the dog-eat-dog world of adolescent girls, she is the outlier, the weird one, the one who doesn't flirt with mascara and boys. Conformity is everything in 1976 San Diego, the hall pass to group acceptance, and Libby is the nail that sticks out.

No Dittos jeans with saddleback yokes or feathered Farrah Fawcett hair for her. She wears a crumpled driving cap on her short blonde hair, thin and crunchy green from the swim team, and gingham bell-bottoms, a maroon-white pair one day, a blue-white pair the next. With a chipmunk face and thunder thighs, also thanks to the swim team, specifically the breaststroke, Libby is indifferent to popularity and the social moves that garner it. I've known her since the fifth grade and have never talked to her.

Three months before ninth grade begins, Libby shows up in my summer school typing class, the only person I know in the room. Teenage jungle aside, she is my best option, better than sitting next to a stranger or, worse yet, alone.

"Hi," I say, approaching her at a shiny black table set up with two Smith Coronas.

Early morning sun streams in the big louvered windows, and part cat, I angle my seat toward Libby so that the rays warm my back.

"Hi," she grins the first time we ever interact, apparently the forgiving type.

"Why are you taking a typing class?" I ask.

"My mom is making me. She thinks it'll help me get a job later."

Libby sounds embarrassed, whether by her mother or the idea of a typing job, I can't tell. "Why are you?"

"I thought it sounded fun," I shrug. "And I like school."

Libby's blue eyes dance, and she laughs.

"What?" I scowl. "What's so funny?"

"You're taking a summer school class for fun!" she says, as though it's obvious.

"Yeah . . . so what?" I roll my eyes, not getting the joke.

"Nothing." She stops grinning, but her eyes still dance. "I mean, I guess you're really smart."

I check to see if she's making fun of me, but she seems sincere, a little admiring even. And our friendship is born, the best and worst turn of my young life. Five days a week, for six weeks, we tap out asdfjkl; and Good children can have dessert and The forest is very dark and cool. Between drills, we talk.

With other girls, girls I want to like me, I hide the intense, serious, you-think-too-much parts of myself that my mother says make people uncomfortable. Libby, on the other hand, means nothing to me. This is summer school, and I don't care what she thinks. I'm real for the first time ever because, for the first time ever, I have nothing to lose. Long before my wisdom catches up, the power of living my truth begins to work its magic. Libby likes me. She really likes me. And I like her. She's fun and laid-back, funny and real. Her solitariness intrigues me, a salmon swimming not upstream but in a transverse flow. Before long, we are bike-riding, movie-going, mall-shopping friends.

We race to the beach—green Stingray for me, red Schwinn ten-speed for her—along smooth, wide roads lined with striking homes, emerald lawns, and magenta bougainvillea that will one day be featured in Architectural Digest and Better Homes and Gardens. The sparkling blue ocean kicks up its salt mist at the edge of fine, white sand where we lay out in baby oil, the SPF of our day.

Summer's highlight, the hours-long and thrillingly patriotic Fourth of July parade, teems with prancing, dancing horses in colorful ribbons to match their riders; military brass and marching bands; and decommissioned tanks and bombers with their wings folded up, too wide at full extension to pass through the crowd.

Libby and I, too, for a time are innocent and untroubled. The storm is not yet on the horizon.

The earth tilts on its axis, bathing us in elongated rays of diffuse, mellow sunshine, San Diego's only hint of fall, and a new school year begins. Sprinkled among the high school's low-slung buildings are offspring of movie stars, war heroes, and ambassadors. Libby and I, more common-variety offspring, flutter like happy butterflies. It's as close to silly as I get, and I like it. I like Technicolor. I like happy. There's no going back to my flat, black-and-white world.

I've tried so hard to brighten my mother's world, tried so hard to make her happy so that I can be happy. I'm obedient, polite, eat my vegetables, do my chores. For her birthday when I was ten, I made lamb with mint jelly, my first gourmet meal. It didn't work. Nothing I do makes her happy. She doesn't smile or spend time with me. Lonely, I draw more deeply from Libby, her attention an unfamiliar and heady feeling that lifts me out of my no-win situation.

Imperceptibly, the skies begin to darken.

I wear the IZOD shirts and bright white K-Swiss tennis shoes that she does. I cut my hair and join the swim team. We are inseparable. I like her house better, although I don't like her mother, a divorced woman who calls Libby "Missy" in a loud, gravelly voice and bosses her around. I like my mother less; her eyes are hard when she sees Libby, and her smile brittle, only technically polite. Neither house is comfortable, neither mother welcoming. After school and every weekend, we run the gauntlet to our own private world behind the bedroom door.

October in San Diego is hot and dry, the heavy scent of fading roses lifted up on Santa Ana winds that whip in from the desert. On a staticky Friday night, not two months before the death of our friendship, emotional lightning cracks the sky. At Libby's house tonight, our giggles start like every other sleepover. Nothing stands out; nothing prepares us for an end more menacing than cartoons and soggy corn flakes. But something tonight is different, some culmination of the ache for love that overwhelms me, its momentum collapsing the boundary between us with an exhilarating whoosh.

"Why don't you ever kiss me?" I ask, blissfully unaware of religious prohibition, psychiatric diagnosis, or the oncoming tempest.

Libby, with what must be similar yearning, gently touches her lips to mine: my first kiss. In all the years to come, in all the dizzying variety of physical intimacy I will experience, nothing will erase the feeling of that kiss. It is vulnerable in the way that first kisses are—pure, free from comparison to any other kiss. We flow together easily, satisfaction filling us in deep, humming waves. Golden, soothing tenderness eases into my aching, more powerful than any drug I will ever ingest, the original high I will be chasing in all future substances. The etchings on our souls have found a match.

We break apart just long enough to search each other's face, and, finding only pleasure, touch our lips again. We kiss a long time that night. We kiss even longer the next. Not a word passes between us. For once, I don't need to analyze.

The first before and after of my life has taken place. Libby's eyes, the window to her soul, reflect the change I feel inside myself, an upwelling of strength and confidence. To be wanted is powerful, an impact never undone no matter what the aftermath. Nothing, most especially me, will ever be the same, a blurry truth I grasp like the edges of a dream.

Storm clouds begin to glower darkly above, but, besotted with affection and physical warmth, we don't notice. We know enough to hide it; some things are instinctual. Instinctive, too, are other things, fervently exciting, fervently disconcerting things. The rules meant to constrain girls with boys, the precepts meant to guard if not preserve their innocence, are nonexistent between girls in a bedroom, unsupervised. There is no going back from this either. I tumble in a whirl no thirteen-year-old can process alone.

We need each other to breathe. We get passes from our classes and meet in the girls' restroom to kiss. The smokers in need of their own hiding place, hard-edged versions of both celebrity and common-variety girls, find us again and again, our faces hot with almost detection.

First a sprinkling, then a cold, steady rain begins to pelt us from all sides; rumors, rough looks, vulgar gestures. I pretend not to notice. Everything is fine, says my solid, determined walk down the turquoise-lockered halls, eyes straight ahead, blood pounding in my ears.

I ignore the snickers, the "Hey, DOG-na, too ugly to get a guy?"

A funnel cloud of rumors touches down a few days after my fourteenth birthday. Mrs. Hinton, our perpetually tan swim team coach, calls me down to her office where she sits at her desk in white shorts and a short-sleeved polo shirt. A peculiar foreshadowing of things to come, she is Mormon, the only adult who ever reaches out to me.

I see Libby inside, and I know it's going to be bad. A cold wave rolls up my spine, and my chest tightens. My upper lip breaks out in sweat while in my stomach, the clenched fist that will be my constant companion for the next twenty-five years, slowly squeezes the air out of my lungs.

Mrs. Hinton looks back and forth between us as though deciding something. Her voice when she speaks is matter-of-fact but not unkind.

"Girls, you need to make other friends. People are talking about you."

Burning heat rushes to the top of my scalp. I feel sick, and the air is tight around me. She doesn't explain why people are talking about us, and we don't ask, all of us complicit in the conversation that isn't really conversation. Libby, intensely studying her K-Swiss, says nothing. Survival mode, familiar to me as Sunday dinner, kicks in. I pull a garish slash across my face, meant to be a smile, and try to still my trembling cheeks. If Mrs. Hinton notices, she doesn't say.

"Thanks, Mrs. Hinton, we will," I manage, a little breathlessly over the wild thumping in my chest.

I have to drop my gaze as soon as the words are out. The shame I've carried for so long, layer upon layer of magical thinking that blames myself for all my unmet needs, is doused in the kerosene of gossip. It is Mrs. Hinton's unwillingness to name the thing, her tacit inference that it is too shameful to name, that sparks the match. Shame feeds on itself as shame so often does, and pretending everything is fine, that I am fine, hardens into steel. I have no idea, rooted there under the yellowy fluorescent lights, how badly I will need this armor to survive, or the price it will exact.

Mrs. Hinton dismisses us with a nod and a "Good girls."

I scurry away, face hot, in the opposite direction from Libby, both of us rats on a sinking ship. We do what we're told. We don't meet in the restroom anymore. We don't even look at each other in the hall. I try to make other friends, go back to other friends, but I can't, weighted down with the slow burning agony of wondering who knows and what they think. What are they saying about me behind my back? It's a slippery slope. If I'm pretending, maybe they are, too. I don't trust anyone. I will have a hard time trusting friendships ever again.

The high school rumor mill is as old as the hills and twice as prolific when it comes to sex. Kids I don't know harass me at my locker. Only a passing acquaintance with truth is required and not even that once the mill is up and running. One of the rumors, a mild bit of swim team truth mingled with the philosophy of romance, is hardest for me to take.

Four girls press around me at my locker.

"Heard you were singing to your girlfriend on the bus," snickers Ponytail.

I maintain my head-down, eyes-down stance.

"I don't sing!"

I never sing. I don't even like to talk. My voice is so low pitched that callers mistake me for my father on the phone. My voice, which will one day be decidedly sultry under the right circumstances, is, to me, ugly and unfeminine. I know that's why boys have called me DOG-na since third grade. The sharp pain is bone deep.

"Yeah," Ponytail continues, "they said you were singing 'You Are So Beautiful' on the way to the swim meet and looking into each other's eyes."

"Yeah! You are sooooo beautiful," one of the other girls sneers, and they all laugh.

My head snaps up.

"I did not!" I practically yell, but they are already walking away.

The rumor is out there, and there's nothing I can do to stop it, just like all the other rumors, even the true ones. My happiness is gone. Things are still in Technicolor, but I'm living in a goldfish bowl. When we aren't in school, Libby and I cling to each other more than ever, deflating like a blow-up doll with a slow leak.

In a move that sets the tragic final events in motion, I make the fateful decision to give her a key to our pistachio-green rambler, and ask her to wake me up in the mornings with kisses. My mother might be a drinker, but she is no fool. She catches us the first time Libby lets herself in.

TWO

"Every man has his secret sorrows which the world knows not;
and oftentimes we call a man cold when he is only sad."
—HENRY WADSWORTH LONGFELLOW

I may have a low-pitched voice and my father's masculine underbite, a defect one day to be corrected by reconstructive jaw surgery, but my bedroom is all girl. Decorated entirely by my mother in wishful thinking, the room is a pink-bedecked extravaganza—pink walls, pink ceiling, pink scalloped bedspread, and the tie-it-all-together feature: light-and-dark pink shag carpet.

Unsated by the matchy-matchy bedroom, or perpetually hopeful, she has continued the same theme down the hall into the bathroom with its own pink walls and ceiling, pink toilet seat, pink-tiled shower—relieved only barely around the edges by a tiny row of turquoise—and a thick, pink vinyl shower curtain trimmed in pink fuzzy balls that stretch across the top. It could not be less me.

When Libby sneaks into my room, having slipped into the house with our spare key, I am still under the covers, sleepy and warm, so happy to see her. She tiptoes to the bed as though it's the noise of her footsteps that might betray us rather than the heavy door creak a moment ago. Teenagers are nothing if not short on logic. She folds one leg underneath her and leans against me in the twin bed, a Sears and Roebuck special with tiny pink roses and gold trim on the ornately carved princess headboard.

Sears had mistakenly delivered a set of mahogany bunk beds, and I had begged my mother to keep them, but her vision for my bedroom was nonnegotiable. The vision my mother is about to see will be nonforgettable.

Libby grins down at me, the same happy grin from typing class. We are in bliss, pure, unadulterated bliss, achingly unaware that it is the last time we will ever smile at each other. A magnetic force pulls the softness of her mouth to mine, as it always does; the pleasure of kissing grown stronger with the deepening of our bond and affection. I wonder dimly if this is what happy babies feel: swaddled, cuddled, nourished, and cherished. There isn't a wish or a need in my whole, deeply satisfied world.

Suddenly I smell Chanel No. 5 and look up. I wish I hadn't. I wish I'd never met Libby. I wish the flooding heat in my brain would burn me mercifully unconscious. Instead, the ferocious vision of spots I blink so furiously to clear away stands motionless in the doorway—my mother in her leopard-print bathrobe. I shove Libby away from me and scrabble frantically to piece together what my mother saw, what she thinks, what she'll do.

"Go home, Libby!" commands the leopard in a voice that leaves no room for doubt. She saw, she knows.

Powdered, rouged, and lipsticked for work, my mother's hair is sculpted in small green curlers set in tight rows along her crown and down each side of her face. I catch only a flash of the queasy set of her mouth as I lock onto the fuzzy blanket, pink of course, around my knees. On the inside, I writhe like Medusa's snakes; on the outside, I study blanket fuzz balls.

Poor Libby thinks my mother has said, "No more," not, "Go home," so she sits there, frozen, terrified of what the leopard will do next.

"Go home, Libby!" The shrill ugliness in my mother's voice clears up any confusion.

Libby flattens past my mother in the doorway and is gone. So is everything else. The full raging storm has hit and will leave nothing standing, not me, not my friendship with Libby, not my ability to connect emotionally to myself or anyone else, not my parents' marriage.

I will not see Libby again for six months, and by then we will be strangers. She is sent away to private school by her gravelly-voiced mother after a phone call from the leopard. When she returns at the beginning of sophomore year, we will pass each other again and again in the turquoise-lockered halls, eyes averted, graduating without contact of any kind. Behind a face of carefully masked anguish, I will pretend fiercely, as a matter of survival, that I don't even know her.

Living my lie in the goldfish bowl is meant to spare me the rubbed-raw state of being strafed by so many watchful eyes. The strain scorches my mind's inner workings, perforating a fragile trapdoor to emotional instability. Like my mother, I will dance at the edges of self-control, self-destruction, and self-doubt. Unlike her, I will never plunge through completely, a nod to my father's genetic contribution, or the hand of God, or both.

But that is all to come. The storm has only begun to rage, its ragged litter not yet deposited into every cranny of my life. In this moment, I am still face-to-face with the leopard, nothing between us now but a sea of light-and-dark pink shag. Dark anger and even darker disgust cascades off my mother in waves, met by my own sure knowledge that Libby's affection saved my life. Humans survive. It is what we do, calling it to ourselves in countless instinctive, usually unconscious, often brilliant ways. Because of Libby, I have been nurtured, the vision without which I would perish but with which I will know what to seek from here on.

My mother finally speaks, the ugliness in her voice still present if less shrill. "What the hell do you think you're doing?"

"Nothing," I mutter, the classic teenage response.

It will take almost three decades and a fair amount of humbling by my own reprehensible behavior, but I will one day find a tender if surprising compassion for my mother in this bedroom scene. I will think back to what must have been her complete unpreparedness to face what was, in her time, a universally acknowledged perversion in her own daughter. No Dr. Phil to help her, no Oprah, no Internet, no support groups.

I will never forget her question to me soon after, almost heartbreaking in its hopefulness: "Do lesbians marry gay men?"

Touched by her need to know, moved by her guilelessness, my voice will be gentle when I answer, "No, Mom, no, they don't. That's the point."

This early morning in my bedroom, she is flying blind, probably a bit inebriated as well, and I am in survival mode—standard operating procedure.

If she is a leopard, I am a crocodile, my eyes closed to mere slits. I intend to slither ever so stealthily through the coming spate of judgments, exposing nothing more of myself. The unfurling trauma that will haunt me the rest of my life takes shape in those first few moments of my mother standing in the doorway, shaking her green plastic curlers in disgust. The humiliating flash that exposed my—to her eyes—depravity, leaves mottled spots of shame behind on my vulnerability, a stain I will never fully expunge.

I stare at my pink ocean and wait.

"Well, no more!" my mother growls. "No more! Do you hear me?"

"Yes, ma'am," I answer, relieved that no further discussion will take place.

It is a sickly feeling to be dependent on someone not capable of leading. My mother always said I raised myself, but she thought she was joking. If, in fact, I am raising myself, I'm not doing a very good job. I should be sitting down with myself to have The Talk.

I should say something like, "Honey, these feelings and desires you have for love and intimacy are God-given and beautiful, but there is a right time and a right place to express them."

Instead, I pretend that nothing has happened. I'm fine, things are fine—a tough act to render but I manage. With Libby's disappearance from school, the crush at my locker becomes a feeding frenzy.

"Where's your girlfriend?"

"Did'ya get her pregnant?"

"When's the baby due?"

"Come on, DOG-na, you can tell us!"

They all high-five each other thinking they are so, so hilarious. The familiar heat flushes up my neck and head. I study my locker combination, pretending I can't hear them; with the blood roaring in my ears, I really can't, a tiny tender mercy. I never cry. They never break me. My smooth, steely, outside is indifferent to it all. Inside, the writhing snakes leave me bruised and shaky. I am falling, and there is no one to catch me.

At home, we keep to the code: no personal conversation. Neither my mother nor I ever bring up The Incident, and I assume my father is not aware since his communication toward me, or lack thereof, remains the same. He settles behind his newspaper in the blue velvet chair next to the bank of living room windows, completely obscured from the knees up—my strongest memory of him—never deviating from his after-work routine or any other routine for that matter.

He makes hot cereal every morning—oatmeal, cream of wheat, or Malt-O-Meal, leaving the pan warming on the stove in a tin pie plate filled with water, the depression-era survivor's double boiler, until my sister and I are ready for breakfast. He washes the dishes, alone, every night after dinner and then makes our lunches for school: peanut butter and marshmallow cream sandwiches, chips, and only half a fruit pie, whether because he is conserving resources or because I already shop in the chubby department at Sears, I don't know. Thursday is grocery-shopping day, Saturday is for yard work, and on Sunday, he serves as deacon in our church.

The change in tension, and it is only a matter of degree, comes from my mother who retreats further into her yellow coffee mug, spending more time in her cave of a dark-green bedroom with the shades drawn. The slouchy beanbag chair in the television room, the one that smells of potato chips and loneliness, is my only friend, the only protection from the tension behind me. Every cell in my body is trained in my mother's direction, waiting for the inevitable explosion. It comes in waves.

"I'm going to take you to Doctor Fader tomorrow," she says one morning on her way out the door to work.

"Yes, ma'am," answers the crocodile; no questions, no comments, no provocation. But I have no idea who Dr. Fader is, or why I need him. Dr. Fader, it turns out, is a psychiatrist; the very psychiatrist who, with my father, committed my mother against her will when I was three and administered electroshock therapy. My mother brings me to his stuffy, overheated office in downtown San Diego and waits in the lobby for him to cure me.

I know nothing of the Diagnostic and Statistical Manual (DSM) or its classification of homosexuality as mental illness, the removal of which only three years previously had been met with fierce opposition by numerous psychiatrists, perhaps even Dr. Fader.

Adolescence is an age imbued with the dichotomy of shame and defiance. We can defend almost any behavior while twisting in mortification at the same time. I had known to hide my relationship with Libby, but standing alone on the rubble of my life, I refuse to admit I've done anything wrong.

The weekly sessions with Dr. Fader are not productive, in part because he is not gifted with adolescents. They all run the same course.

Dr. Fader: How are you doing today?
Donna: This is a waste of my father's money. I didn't do anything wrong.
Dr. Fader: (Various questions.)
Donna: (Silence to all questions.)
Dr. Fader: Our time is up.
Donna: Do I have to come back?
One week, finally, he says, "No."

What findings Dr. Fader is able to obtain come from my mother's data alone. She is quick to report his diagnosis: negative self-image causing patient to turn to a woman. She doesn't mention whether he places any of the responsibility on her or my father, or the lack of relating, let alone nurturing, in our home. I feel like a dreamer screaming without sound.

While the baby-bear wave of the explosion rolls on, the mama-bear wave begins. My father, still crisp in his white shirt and tie from work, comes to my bedroom one night before Christmas. No matter how long my father stays dressed after work, he never loosens his tie or rolls up his sleeves. He awkwardly lowers his six-foot-three frame to the studio couch beside my desk where my bright-yellow lamp, the only other color in the room, shines a neat round circle onto my Algebra textbook.

My father in my bedroom with something to say is surreal. It would be exciting but for the fist in my gut that tells me something awful is coming. I know already that it is about me and Libby.

"I'm going to be moving out," he says in his deep voice that embarrasses me when he sings at church because it's so much lower than everyone else's.

A sharp nausea rips through my stomach, and I stare at my homework. His words hang in the two-and-a-half-dimensional space. I'm going to be moving out. Inside the lamp's warm circle, I make small dots on my book with a pencil. If I don't look at him, maybe he will take it back. When I don't speak, he continues.

"Mommy blames me for what happened with Libby. She says I wasn't affectionate enough with you when you were growing up. She doesn't want me to do the same thing to your sister that I did to you."

My dark brown eyes seek his own. I'm so confused. How can he go back and fix what he's done to my sister when she's already eleven? I look down again, humiliated that my father knows about my degenerate needs for affection. Then a horrible, terrible, awful thought presents itself. My mind closes on a picture of me alone with my mother. I rush up toward his face again.

"Can I come with you?"

The plaintive sound of my voice makes me feel small. He won't leave me alone with her, will he? Somehow I already know that he will. The expression on his face is unreadable.

"Please, Daddy?" My heart shudders, but still he doesn't answer. "Daddy?"

It's getting hard to breathe. Hot, salty tears slip into my mouth. When he speaks, it is classic Daddy, no emotion.

"No, you stay here." He looks down at his hands.

"I don't want to stay here!" I yelp, scalded.

My father's eyes flash quickly in the direction of my mother's bedroom.

"You stay here," he repeats quietly, looking again down the hallway.

"Why? Why do I have to stay? I don't want to stay!"

I can see my train leaving the station, can see that I won't make it, but I keep running anyway. I run even though I know he can't take me with him. He can't afford to upset my mother. He knows better than anyone how fragile she is. He stands up, crisp as ever, our only meaningful interaction in fourteen years at an end.

"You need to stay here."

Then he is gone, too. I make more pencil dots on my book. Keep it together, I tell myself, keep it together, keep it together. Somehow I do. I always do.

The papa-bear wave is the worst. I am setting the table for dinner a week later, only three places now, when my father opens the sliding glass door from the patio into the kitchen, as handsome as ever. My mother, a secretary, still striking at forty-seven, is dressed in her work clothes, a pumpkin-colored skirt set that brings out her blue eyes and dark hair. She hates cooking, hates having to think of what to cook, and stands at the stove irritably clanging pots. When she sees my father, she erupts.

"What do you want?"

"I need some shirts," he answers meekly.

"You said you took everything you needed! You can't just show up here when you feel like it!"

My mother slams a lid on the counter and turns back to the stove. My father holds still, waiting in the well-worn what-will-upset-her-least pose.

She whips around again.

"What are you waiting for? Go get your shirts!"

Dark splotches break out on her face, the same hue as her suit.

Head down, my father strides quickly to what had been their bedroom for seventeen years. I assume the crocodile position, as invisible as possible, finishing the table as quietly as possible. My mother clangs and slams and mutters in rising agitation the longer my father is gone. With his first step back into the kitchen, his arms full of shirts, she launches at me like a tightly wound spring suddenly shot from its coil. She stops abruptly just inches from my face; the alcohol on her breath barrels into me. My throat seizes up, and I can't look away. Her eyes radiate a dark, crazy heat. She leans in even closer.

"And you!" She puts so much dripping disgust on the "you," I think she might spit. "You make me sick!"

Lightening quick, the crocodile strikes and slaps my mother's face. No thought goes into my instinctive defense; it is pure fight or flight. She rears back, and I clap my horrified hands to my mouth, echoes of the slap fading in the shock between us. I feel the warm softness of her cheek on the hand that stings from how hard I hit her. She looks, surprisingly, calmer, but I am ablaze with panic.

I am in another dream now, a dream where I've slapped my own mother. This can't be real. I look to my father for something, anything, but he stands fixed in the doorway, as silent after my slap as he was after her explosion. The trapdoor in my mind beckons. How easy it would be to let myself slip through, leaving my overwhelming reality behind.

Flight takes over, and I break for the sliding glass door, so heavy I need both hands to pull it open. I run to the white patio gate with its peekaboo slats and try frantically to lift it over years of Podocarpus tree roots that have buckled the concrete. Bracing every second for an angry hand on my neck, I struggle until adrenaline finally bests the gate.

I fly down the driveway in my K-Swiss, past the quiet ramblers on our street where happy families hug and play games.

I run even though there is nowhere to go—no friends, no neighbors, no relatives, no teachers, no pastor, no therapist, no sibling, no parent I can trust. I have no idea what to do. The thought ricochets through my frenzied brain. I don't know how to fix this. Nearly hysterical, the thought sears me. I have nowhere to go. I can't go back. I race through the gathering dark, trying to outrun my panic, trying not to fall through the perforated door in my mind.

Eventually, more out of exhaustion than resolution, I circle back in an aimless, miserable walk. Streetlamps pour yellow cones of light into the jasmine-scented evening, and through the shadows, I'm stunned to see my father heading toward me. I can't imagine why. When I was six, he taught me to ride a bike; once he hit some tennis balls with me; and a week ago he told me he was moving out. That's it. Those are the only times I can remember him talking to me in my entire life. I stop and wait, watching to see what he will do.

When he reaches me, his face is tight, his jaw is set, and he doesn't meet my eyes. He takes my arm firmly, and without speaking, leads me back to my mother's house. I let him, defeated. His shiny shoes make regular tap tap tap sounds on the sidewalk next to my silent, shamed K-Swiss. At the top of the driveway, he guides me through the still wide-open patio gate and through the sliding glass door into the kitchen. I close my eyes knowing the hell I'm about to catch. And deserve.

My mother stands at the counter, her back to both of us, chopping carrots so violently that the blade sticks in the cutting board with each strike. She jerks it out and slams it down, jerks it out, slams it down. I wait for her to turn around, to cry, to yell, to punish me. She never does. She doesn't speak. She doesn't look at me. I look at my father to see that he, too, is watching her. It dawns on me that we are all going to pretend it didn't happen. The Incident, like all incidents, will be denied conversation and healing.

Until the day I move out three and a half years later, we will not speak, my mother and I, except to pass the salt, accomplish chores, or negotiate school supplies, clothes, and paperwork. She and her coffee mug will live in her bedroom cave. I and my junk food will live in the beanbag chair watching The Mary Tyler Moore Show; Charlie's Angels; One Day at a Time; Welcome Back, Kotter; The Love Boat; Mork & Mindy; The Bob Newhart Show; The Six Million Dollar Man; The Waltons; Dallas; I Love Lucy; The Carol Burnett Show; Sonny & Cher; and Donny & Marie.

At school I hide, or think I do, behind a chinkless exterior. From K-Swiss and IZOD shirts, I switch hastily to stiletto Candie's, pencil skirts with long slits, and blue mascara. Like extreme pressure on carbon turns it into diamond, the crush on my insides turns me sparkly on the outside. I glitter with half a dozen AP classes, a silver medal for backstroke in the Junior Olympics, piano recitals, advancement to the county spelling bee, three part-time jobs at once, the California Honor Society, and, ultimately, acceptance to UC Berkeley.

The new, more glamorous me produces no real results to speak of. The one time a boy asks me out—my mother lets a senior take me to his prom while I am still a freshman—is not long after Libby leaves, and he is clearly titillated by the rumors. Four years older and fifty pounds heavier, he pushes for certain extras during the night that I am unwilling to provide. Luckily for me, he accepts my refusal and brings me home early. I never hear from him again.

An interminable series of days, weeks, months, and years crawl by as I harden, dead from the neck down. I keep everyone at arm's length. Although some seem sincere in their friendship, I can't trust it, always wondering what they know and what they think. I don my Ray-Bans, flip my hair, and drink my Tab.

As sunrise dawns on my post-graduation life, I fly toward it on wings of hope that things will be different. In the innocence of youth, I think that to leave something behind means to be done with it forever. In the wisdom of age, I will realize that those delicate and jagged etchings on my soul were flying with me.

THREE

"What strange places our lives can carry us to, what dark passages."
—JUSTIN CRONIN
The Passage

France. Land of fine wine, delicious food, rich culture, and great art. Also, as I am soon to discover, its own share of dysfunctional families. Slipped between sunset on home and sunrise on Berkeley is a long night in France as an exchange student—365 days of the most bizarre experiences I will ever have. Afterward, when I am back to tell the story, people will ask why I stayed. I stay because pretending things are fine is what I do.

"Happy families are all alike; every unhappy family is unhappy in its own way," says Tolstoy in Anna Karenina. Coming from one uniquely unhappy family, I will meet and live with two uniquely unhappy French families in my year there. My mother once said, it seemed to me rather defensively,

"Every family is dysfunctional." I remember resenting the idea, as though she were excusing the dysfunction in our family when I wanted her to take responsibility for it. After my experiences in France, I will wonder if she is right.

It all starts off well enough, arriving in Paris with a group of twenty American teenagers in July of 1980. The organization responsible for coordinating our host families wants us to have a quintessentially French experience our first night and takes us to see a live production of Les Misérables. I understand not a word, a bad sign I think. In hindsight, it may have been a bad omen as well.

My first host family and, if things had gone according to plan, what would have been my only host family, lives just outside Montauban, a medieval red-brick town about an hour south of Toulouse, not far from the border with Spain. My host family has sent a daughter abroad the same year I am to live with them; like me she is seventeen and will be spending her exchange student year in New York. I am settled into her sunny bedroom overlooking the garden.

A heretofore unquestioned policy in the exchange-student organization has allowed my new family, the Barniers, to receive me into their home without so much as a screening simply because they have sent a child abroad via the same organization. This will prove to be a serious misjudgment, and my experience with them will spell a hasty end to said policy.

Colette and Bernard Barnier are simple folk, far from my fantasy of the stylish, sophisticated Europeans I've nurtured through six years of junior high and high school French.

Bernard's thick rug of chest hair protrudes over the neck of his tank top, which, because of his large belly, protrudes over his too-tight, too-short shorts. Colette's bouffant hair, cat-eye glasses, and scarf tied under her chin evoke the black-and-white women of I Love Lucy.

They work a small farm with the help of two swarthy young men from town, men who yet again seem to have no interest in me, despite my blue mascara, high-heeled Candie's, and an at-last slimmed-down physique.

The Barniers are good to me. Colette teaches me to make French pastry, and Bernard reads me stories from the local newspaper, helping me to practice the language I will live in for the next twelve months. I can't wait to start school, looking forward to showing off a little as I repeat my senior year of high school at the local lycée. Finally mine, I hope, will be the carefree school experience I'd lost through all the humiliation with Libby. Picturing myself the object of flattering attention as l'Américaine, my thoughts ripple happily along until the afternoon I find Bernard lying on my bed.

"Come here, chérie," he calls. "Come lie beside me."

I go stiff, and a sickening apprehension floods my belly, squeezing its way up into my chest. I work at keeping my face impassive, a slight crocodile adaptation, while alarm bells go off in my brain.

"Non, merci," I chirp brightly and back out the door.

Pretending nothing is wrong works with magical, circular effect. If I don't react with alarm, it normalizes the behavior in question, and normalizing makes it feel normal, nothing to be alarmed about. Still, a forty-something man wanting me to lie on a twin bed with him only days after meeting requires some action on my part.

I locate Colette in the kitchen and, keeping my voice as light as possible, ask, "Why is Bernard lying on my bed?"

"He and our daughter lie there together listening to music. He wants you to feel like part of the family."

She smiles sweetly at me, clearly sincere.

"Oh, that's nice," I lie.

A bad feeling, odious and sour, slides over me from head to toe. I know this is not okay, at least I think I do. I'm not the best judge of healthy boundaries in a family. What is certain is that I am seven thousand miles away from anyone or anything familiar and isolated on a farm without the ability to communicate fully.

Pretending takes on almost life-or-death importance, a Stockholm syndrome allegiance to the people I depend on for survival. The hope I brought with me, that things would be better once I left home, evaporates. I focus on making the Barniers think I'm happy, grateful for their hospitality. Pastry instruction and newspaper reading continue, and I casually make excuses to avoid Bernard in my bedroom. I am almost comfortable with this new layer of pretending, a hardening of my survival mask that actually makes me feel safer, when Colette presents a new challenge: she doesn't like it that I don't eat meat.

Californians are often the vanguard of new trends, especially those of an ecological or new age nature; I am not one of them. My only reason for not eating meat is that the idea of eating a dead body makes me ill. Colette, however, cannot accept this anathema to farm life. First she tries sneaking meat into my food.

"Donna," (pronounced Dough-NAH), "how do you like the casserole?" Colette beams.

"It's very good, merci," I answer politely and truthfully.

"Aha! I put a little meat in there! You see, you like meat! You're not a vegetarian!"

"Yes, I am!" I push my plate away, stung by the trick and unnerved that I have just eaten flesh.

I thereafter surreptitiously inspect my food before I eat it, removing any meat to my napkin as discreetly as possible. Colette is not fooled.

Outside at the rabbit hutch a few days later, she calls to me. "Come here, Donna, I want you to see something."

She holds up a small brown lapin with quivering whiskers and velvety soft fur. I stroke lightly down the rabbit's back not wanting to scare it, but Colette pushes my hand away.

"Non!" she says.

Gripping the soft folds behind its neck like a cat would hold its kitten, Colette plunges a knife into the rabbit's throat and twists, releasing a small river of blood down its jerking body. I am in yet another dream, a horrific nightmare, my eyes fixed in a stranglehold on the now-still rabbit hanging limp in Colette's hand, its fur matted with quickly darkening blood. The sight and the smell make me want to vomit, but she is oblivious to my distress.

"You see, Donna," Colette says with her sweet smile, "this is what we do in the country. We kill animals, and we eat them."

I nod dumbly. I don't know what else to do. My mask hardens further. I shrink even deeper into myself and let Colette win. I will eat meat now. How I manage it, I'm not sure, except that pretending works in both directions; I fool myself almost as much as I fool anyone else.

Like a frog placed in cold water and cooked while the heat slowly increases, I am lulled by my own pretending that the first two incidents are anything other than freakish. The third incident, however, is so ludicrous that the temperature rockets up past all ability to normalize. Even I, after a few more weeks of my most strenuous efforts to make everything okay, will have to jump out of the pot.

Colette accuses me of being pregnant.

Two months of my very long year have passed, and I have not had a period yet. Later in life, when my body's dramatic reactions to stress are a given, it will all become clear. For now I have no explanation when she confronts me. Holding a pair of my underwear from the laundry, Colette snaps off the television in the living room where I am practicing my French by watching the local news.

"Donna, I see no blood on your underwear since you are here. You have no menses, you are pregnant."

Embarrassed heat spreads over my face as she examines my most vulnerable item of clothing. In shades of the old humiliation, I am helpless to stop her.

"Colette!" I say tightly, "I am not pregnant! I can't be," I insist, "I've never been with a boy."

Colette shakes her head vigorously.

"Non, chérie, non! It is not necessary for you to have sexual relations with a man to become pregnant."

In a more conciliatory, almost educational tone, she goes on. "If you have been sitting on a chair where a man has been sitting, or swimming in a pool where a man has been swimming, you can become pregnant."

I stare at her, my mind turning each phrase over and over until I'm sure I've heard correctly. As French goes, these are not difficult words, and after a long moment, I realize that I have indeed understood her meaning. I have no answer, either in French or in English, but I try again anyway.

"Colette, I promise, I am not pregnant!"

She doesn't hear me, or doesn't listen, but carries on.

"We will love you and the baby, bien sûr, but the village will be scandalized. We can't let you start school. You must stay at home until the baby is born."

I have overcome Bernard on my bed by being creative. I have handled if not overcome Colette and the rabbit by giving in to her, eating meat at every meal. With this latest incident, there is no creativity and no giving in that will make me pregnant or her rational. An admixture of panic, horror, and dread strangles my sense of being able to cope.

"Colette, please!" I beg. "I'm not pregnant! Please let me start school!"

"Donna," Colette commands, "you must take a pregnancy test."

Perhaps I'm not rational myself. Perhaps taking a pregnancy test would convince her, but the pitch-black crush in my mind prevents me from seeing that option. I'm filled only with desperation to save myself from something I cannot handle.

"No!" I shout. "I am not going to take a pregnancy test!" and I bolt for my room, which is mercifully vacant for a change.

My plan to avoid Colette and Bernard and to hope, as usual, that pretending nothing is wrong will work, does, at least temporarily. The next morning at breakfast, no one speaks of the pregnancy; we go on as before. This, at least, is familiar.

September arrives with its brilliantly yellowing leaves and school buses trundling hordes of riders back and forth without me. Every few days, I plead with Colette to let me start at the lycée, but she just shakes her head. Yellow becomes orange-and-red October.

One morning at breakfast, Colette surprises me.

"Today we take you into town to buy some new clothes," she says without explanation. "You may start school tomorrow."

Relief overwhelms curiosity as to why she has suddenly changed her mind. See? I tell myself, everything is going to be fine.

"Merci, Colette, oh merci!" I thank her profusely.

It is a family trip into town on gently curving roads marked with the detritus of autumn, Bernard at the wheel of his metallic-gray Citroën CX. When he cuts the engine, however, I notice that rather than a clothing store, he has stopped in front of a building whose sign advertises Gynécologue.

A blow of sick comprehension knocks everything into place: the refusal to let me start school for over a month, the sudden change of heart, the offer to buy me a new outfit first. This isn't about school at all; this is still about a pregnancy test, another trick. The primitive part of my brain, the fight-or-flight instinct given to all creatures, reacts without thought.

Flinging open the car door, I tear down the sidewalk, ignoring the Barniers' angry shouts behind me. As I run, something I will later come to believe is God's hand over my life lifts my attention to a large stone building on the right carved with the words Bureau de Poste. The thought comes into my mind, You can make a collect call from the post office. I don't remember knowing that before. I don't know how I know it now, but I hurtle through the massive front doors in frantic search of a phone.

Along the side wall is a row of empty cabines téléphoniques. Scrambling into the first one, I slam the pleated door closed and grab the receiver. I dial "0" and drop into a crouch at the bottom of the booth, terrified that Bernard and Colette will find me. I am panting so hard, as much from panic as running, that the operator can hardly understand my jumbled French.

"Excusez-moi?" she asks sharply.

"I said, s'il vous plaît, please help me! I need to call Paris!"

I have no phone number for the agency that placed me with Colette and Bernard, but the operator is able to connect me rather quickly on a collect call.

"Bonjour," says a female voice.

"My name is Donna," I pant, still in a frenzy. "You placed me with a family here! I can't go back! You have to come get me! Please!"

"Shhhh, it weel be oh-kay, Donna," she says soothingly. "I weel help you. Where are you?"

"I'm at the post office in Montauban in a phone booth. Can you come get me now? They're going to find me!"

I squeeze back tears, alone and trembling in a foreign world, now dependent on a reassuring stranger at the other end of a phone for survival. The minimal composure I've maintained throughout the whole ordeal begins to thin as I sense her compassion. Falling apart is an unfamiliar luxury, only possible now because she is there, whoever she is.

The woman gathers basic information from my mumbled responses, tells me to stay where I am, that someone will drive down from the Toulouse office. When she says, "Adieu," I'm too scared to stand up and replace the receiver in case Colette and Bernard see me. I let it hang, bracing my feet against the door to keep them out, my will the only thing holding me together.

Some children are born more strong willed than others. Religious-minded parents, who tend to see order and meaning in such things, point to the divine matching of will with trials the child will face in life. On the floor of the phone booth, gripping my head, whether prepared for this trial from birth or only lucky enough to endure it, I refuse to surrender.

When help arrives, one man and one woman, my composure is back. One staff member stays with me at the post office while the other collects my things from the Barnier house. Despite everything that has happened, I feel guilty for leaving. Somehow this is my fault. I don't ask and don't want to know what Colette and Bernard said about me when my belongings were removed, for good, from their home.

My two young rescuers don't speak much during the almost seven-hour drive to Paris. The black Renault, tuned to Radio France, moves steadily down the highway while in the backseat I cut deeper grooves into the now less-delicate etchings. I had been so sure that home was the problem, but in the backseat of the Renault, in a quicksand of shame, I blame myself for every bad thing that has happened since I arrived in France.

It is dusk by the time the car reaches Paris, the city of lights so beautiful, so thrilling to be close to, it sparks my inextinguishable hope that things will be better now. We exit the highway a few minutes later and crunch gravel in the driveway of a small, boxy house. The woman in the passenger seat turns around.

"The familee that leeves here ees veree nice," she tells me. "They weel be your temporaree familee."

Like a foster child, I am placed with Philippe and Caroline Pilon in a rainy, northeast suburb of Paris. They are not a host family but agree to help because their twin daughters are presently exchange students in Iowa. They also have a fifteen-year-old son, Marc, who, I am told, is meant to enjoy this year of attention out from under his sisters' shadow. He looks decidedly unhappy that I am here.

Philippe, mostly gray, slightly soft in the middle, and never far from a wineglass, is meek and soft-spoken. Caroline, the kind of fashionable Frenchwoman I had envisioned, has short, dark hair and small, very white teeth. Her low, breathy voice is delightfully mellifluous until she berates Philippe; then it turns hard and squawky. They will divorce the following year.

Starting the next evening, and every evening for a week, the phone jangles with bad news from the exchange-student organization: they can't find a host family for me, it is too late in the year. Each call ends the same way, impossible not to hear no matter where I am in the tiny house.

"Non! We don't want her! Non! She can't stay!" squawks Caroline night after night.

I can't offer to leave since I have nowhere to go. My hope of better things fades again, the bright light I cling to dimming quickly. I am at the mercy of whatever plan is made for me, and both sides are driving hard. A week later, and I suspect with some financial compensation, Caroline gives in, grudgingly. I am told in no uncertain terms that this is Marc's year, and I am not to bother him or draw attention away from him. My vision of being the exciting l'Américaine goes up in a poof as I make it my business to become as invisible as possible. It is markedly easy given all of my practice. I come out of my room only for school, dinner, and to help with the ironing. The Pilon family does not own a dryer, so clothing, napkins, sheets—everything—must be taken off the clothesline and ironed. Before long, it becomes solely my responsibility, hours of it each day.

School, as had happened in San Diego, becomes my escape. My new friend Laure, already pear-shaped at seventeen, smokes Rothschild cigarettes and wears heavy, blue eyeliner. Under her tutelage, I pluck my eyebrows for the first time, and finally, my parents are galvanized into reaction. I have written home every week detailing Bernard on my bed, the rabbit, the pregnancy test, and the foster family. My parents have simply written back with news of home. Now they are goaded into an actual response.

"Your beautiful eyebrows! What have you done?" my mother writes back after I send home a picture of me in my Camargue boots and black-and-white kaffiyeh. "Your father and I are so disappointed!"

Laure tutors me in the enchantments of smoking as well, which at first aren't enchanting at all. My brand is Marlboro Reds, and the first time I smoke a whole one, I'm so ill I have to lie down. Yet the seductive adolescent cool is enough to outweigh my nausea, and I push forward to acquire the taste. By the time I return to the US, I will be smoking a pack and a half a day. When Caroline finds out that I am smoking, it is c'ést la vie, no big deal. She does not smoke, a rarity among the French, but Philippe smokes Gauloises, short unfiltered cigarettes that reek of Turkish tobacco and go so well with red wine.

A month of ironing later, I turn eighteen, two weeks before Marc turns sixteen. Despite the prohibition against stealing any of his attention, I am invited to celebrate my birthday at his party. There is plenty of smoking and what in America would be called underage drinking. It is my first time tasting alcohol, and in part due to the alcohol and in part due to the ever-deepening etchings, it will also be my first time with a boy.

Finally a boy likes me, I think, confusing what is about to happen with anything remotely personal. Oblivious, like most eighteen-year-olds, to the watchful eyes of others, we slip into my bedroom sometime during the party.

At dinner the next evening, Caroline announces, "Elle a les lèvres usées," an expression to describe my deflowering that is so vulgar, literally, "She has used lips," that I flush with the familiar shameful heat.

It is hard to say whether the birthday party is highlight or lowlight of my year in France. Perhaps it is both. The boy I thought was my boyfriend dumps me when I gain weight over Christmas, and I resume hiding in my bedroom but for the ironing and dinner.

The pink bursting of cherry trees in spring and finally the green of summer herald the countdown for my departure. Giddy and a little careless, I join Philippe one night in his red wine fest. Caroline is out with her lover again, and Philippe unburdens himself. Alcohol flows, Philippe becomes maudlin, and I become intoxicated. Mistaking his openness with me as an invitation to do likewise, I slur a faux pas.

"You've never wanted me here. I'm just the maid. All I do is iron."

The relief at finally being able to speak truth relaxes me even more than the wine.

"Non, non, non, I do want you here. It's Caroline that's the problem," Philippe sympathizes with me. "I'm sorry she is so misérable."

"She is misérable," I petulantly, drunkenly, agree. "I'm glad this is almost over."

The wine gone, I stagger off to my bedroom, a brown and pink cacophony of wallpaper and bedspread that is spinning along with my head. Just before adding a nice Bordeaux accent to the carpet, I pass out on the bed.

Tonight, my junior store of wisdom expands with timeless truth: never give a scorned husband ammunition against his adultering wife. Their shouting wakes me up, and through my throbbing, I recognize Caroline in my room. Cawing something I can't decipher, she grabs my arm and yanks me into a sitting position. I smell cognac's subtle, floral bouquet.

"How dare you say I treat you like la domestique!" Caroline screeches. "After everything I've done for you!" She squeezes my arm harder. "What kind of ungrateful girl are you?"

Another accident of birth, or gift from God depending on your point of view, is crystal-clear mental acuity when threatened. Like perfect pitch, either it is there or it isn't. Under assault from Caroline, my mind turns instantly cloudless and sharp, freed from its drunken sludge; the words line up like soldiers just waiting their turn.

"Oh non, Caroline, I'm so sorry, Philippe must have misunderstood me. I never said you treat me like the maid."

Her grip loosens, and the soldiers march on.

"I'm the one to blame for acting like the maid. I hide behind the ironing. I should give more of myself to you and your family."

Mollified, she lets go of my arm completely.

"Never mind, chérie, sweet dreams," she purrs and exits the bedroom to resume fighting with Philippe, her voice taking up its guttural harshness.

I don't move when she leaves, impressed by my quick reaction to her. France, for all of its turmoil, is a turning point in my self-confidence, both the kind that will take me far in life and the kind that will isolate me from others. It's a proven fact, I tell myself, that I can pretend my way through anything, harden myself against anyone, survive any situation. My traumatized, overconfident-by-way-of-compensation conclusion is that I don't need anyone. I can take care of myself. Dead from the neck down, I convince myself that I can make it entirely on my own. The truth is, I will have to for a long time.

Tension, thick as smoke, permeates the Pilon house in the days that follow, a short six months away from their divorce. My crocodile self circles stealthily from bedroom to ironing board to dinner exactly seventeen more times. I am back in San Diego to watch the televised wedding of Prince Charles and Lady Diana Spencer on July 29, 1981, my only souvenir from France a quickly passing fancy for all things European.

In a month, I will leave for UC Berkeley. The television someone has put in my bedroom while I was gone means I no longer need the slouchy beanbag chair to numb myself with a steady diet of cathode rays. My old distraction just as faithfully shields me from unpleasant reality, like the awful arithmetic that calculates my score as zero for three nurturing families in my first eighteen years.

As day after benumbed day ticks by, that old unquenchable hope rises again that things will be better now, that at college I will unearth the treasure of human connection I crave. Still so blind, still so sadly unaware, I fail to recognize that my unhealed past will shape each attempt.

FOUR

"Life can only be understood backwards;
but it must be lived forwards."
—SOREN KIERKEGAARD

I will never know how things might have gone if I hadn't landed in the all-women's dorm at Berkeley, a four-story, apricot stucco building in the shelter of eucalyptus trees overlooking San Francisco Bay. It may be that the pieces set in motion with Libby are called to make their inevitable next move on the chessboard. Or it may be pure dumb luck that puts me in the same residence hall that lesbians and bisexuals pick on purpose, and that many formerly straight women will find to be their sexual turning point. Either way, two roads diverge in a young girl's life, and the one I find makes all the difference.

Berkeley is like nothing I've seen, a 24/7 carnival of redolent, boisterous humanity. I feel a fullness in my breath, a deep sense of belonging, or maybe it's freedom, that resonates among the kaleidoscope of people, sights, sounds, and smells.

"Hey, man, got a cigarette?"

"Hey, man, got any change?"

"Hey, man, wanna sign a petition?"

"I'll let you spit in my face for a dollar."

I know things are going to be better now. And then I unpack my bags.

I don't like the all-women's dorm by definition—no boyfriend potential. Just blocks away are coed buildings with males layered in between every floor of females. I am stuck with women athletes, soon-to-be sorority girls, and the aforementioned nonheterosexuals, which, paradoxically, both constricts and enhances my sense of belonging and freedom.

Mild panic surges through me when I realize where I am, a recovering alcoholic of sorts in a fully-stocked lesbian bar. I told Dr. Fader I had done nothing wrong, and I believe it. No one can take that away from me. It is, in fact, my Rock of Gibraltar. I may have pretended, but I never surrendered to any of them; they never broke me. Yet it all rests on a sandy foundation because I also believe I am cured. In some kind of complex emotional chemistry that makes no sense, I wasn't sick but now am cured.

Whether I am, whether it's possible, or whether permanent tentacles of humiliation and judgment pull my insides into a scorching twist, I don't want to be here. I barely escaped the wrong I didn't do, and I don't want any more of it. I want a boyfriend, a husband, a white picket fence. I've always wanted those things. I've had a hope chest since I was eight. Libby saved my life, but Libby wasn't the plan.

Like any alcoholic, withdrawal is easier away from the liquor, and surrounded by women-oriented women, I feel the shakes coming on. On one side of the razor's edge are my dreams of an idyllic future with a man; on the other side is the siren call of intimate female nurturing.

The uninitiated may think that it's about sex, or feminism, or even rejection of men, and it may be all of those things. What it's also about, and this is my Achilles' heel, is the depth of bond—some would call it maternal—that's possible between two women. I can't voice the words, won't identify the true need for ages, but I want that bond. I need that bond. It calls to me like the worst kind of drug.

Pretending is what I do. Against a backdrop of dynamic, out-of-the-closet lesbians, I select for my first friend a sure-fire bet, a sorority pledge with a Porsche 930 that we drive up into the hills where her horse is stabled. I attend every rush party with her, trying so hard to feel even half as comfortable as I act. The beer helps, but not enough. The girls are gorgeous. I am not. The guys like sexy. I am not. I feel about as connected to the beautiful people as I do to glossy magazine photos. Even I can't pretend that much, and I give up on Greek life.

My next hope is the boys in my classes, but I must not be gifted in the way of feminine allure. There is one awkward night in my dorm room with a boy whose name I think is David. He apologizes to me the next day for, as he puts it, taking advantage of me, but his regret isn't the kind where he wants to make it up to me. The horizon is empty.

Withstanding a drug can be done, especially if there's an alternative available. When I eventually quit smoking in another five years, I will do it by keeping my hands busy with other things for six months, knitting scarves as Christmas presents for everyone I know. In the all-women's dorm, longing for male attention, I will withstand other, female, opportunities for romantic attention as long as I can, but constant exposure to the ocean of potential all around me eventually wears me down.

It's impossible not to like these girls for one. They are so much more interesting and down-to-earth than the glossy magazine people—finally girls with some edge. Leah, a tough-talking Jew from LA is the alpha, a pacifist in army fatigues and combat boots. PB goes by initials because her given name, translated from the Chinese as Peach Blossom, could not be more radically ill suited to her Mohawk hair and whip-smart math mind. Janet, my favorite, doesn't shave her legs, wear a bra, or go to class, at least not often. Her favorite T-shirt reads, "A Woman Without a Man Is Like a Fish Without a Bicycle."

At first I walk a tightrope of cool friendship. Like I wondered in high school, I wonder here what they think when they look at me. Can they tell? Am I different since I opened that door with Libby? I can close the door, but I wonder if the genie ever goes back in the bottle. A lingering sense of unfemininity dogs me, reinforced by my low-pitched voice, my strong, assertive personality, and the ever-present absence of male interest.

The longer I walk the tightrope, the wearier I become. It was easier to maintain distance with people when I had no choice. The gap between me and these girls is so bridgeable that the undertow of possibility tugs at me constantly. My need to connect, really connect with another human, is the strongest lure of all.

For the first time ever, I talk about Libby, a new before and after.

For almost five years, I have carried it alone. Not a single time, not to a single person have I ever spoken a word of what happened. I never even acknowledged it to those who were there at the time. Released from my solitude, the relief is indescribable. The sympathy, empathy, compassion, and even outrage they show on my behalf is life changing.

There are many who would argue that the God I will find later, the God of the Bible who defines homosexuality as sin, could not be involved in such transformation. I will come to disagree. They have only to read the story of Adam and Eve, commanded by God not to eat of the forbidden fruit when all of God's plan depended upon them doing so. The father in heaven I will eventually come to know knows me already, and knows in perfect wisdom what I need. It is not more judgment. It is the acceptance and unconditional love administered by three human angels named Leah, PB, and Janet. In that moment, heaven touches earth, and the healing that will take me a lifetime has its chance to begin. It is, however, only the tiniest first step in what will remain a rocky, precarious journey.

At first I tell my story for relief, for connection, and as a badge of courage. There is finally space for the hiding, shamed part of me to breathe, to be embraced, a necessary but not sufficient condition of more wholeness. Ironically, it is also my story that plunges the other part of me, the part I'm scared they will reject, into the shadows. They love my story, love that I'm one of them, they think. The only problem is I know I'm not. I want a boyfriend so badly it hurts. Desperate to hold on to their acceptance, terrified they will abandon me if they know, I trade one kind of hiding for another.

Janet is my doorway. We are the most similar of the group, both raised Protestant, both from middle-class backgrounds, both from broken families. There, the similarities end. I am essentially a good girl, obedient, respectful of authority, anxious to please. I never miss class. She is a self-proclaimed anarchist, intent on overthrow of the patriarchy. Brilliant and conversant on almost any subject, she will be kicked out of Cal three years later for essentially submitting no work.

I love the world of ideas in which I have long been denied company, first by my childhood environment, next by the language barrier in France. Janet and I range intellectually and delightfully about life, philosophy, religion, economics, and sexual politics. She holds some of the strangest, most intriguing opinions I've ever encountered, like the idea that God is a woman. That one makes me roll my eyes. It is my first exposure to a religious view that will one day shape my life in powerful ways.

Like me, she is an avid reader and introduces me to counter-culture books like Merlin Stone's When God Was a Woman, Tom Wolfe's The Electric Kool-aid Acid Test, and Aldous Huxley's The Doors of Perception. She also introduces me to drugs.

This before and after isn't as dramatic. My parents have sent me off to Berkeley without any mention of drugs. "Just Say No" is a year away from elementary schools, and D.A.R.E. another seventeen years out. LSD has been illegal in California for only fifteen years, psilocybin mushrooms for ten, and Ecstasy will be legal for another four, so I am almost, not quite but almost, still a good girl. It all starts with marijuana, the ubiquitous gateway drug.

Janet and I have rooms across the hall from each other. My roommate is a pure-as-the-driven-snow type. Janet's roommate commutes home on weekends. Naturally, we spend most of our time in Janet's room. The first time she brings out her pretty jade pipe that she bought on Telegraph Avenue, my stomach clutches. I may not have a formal education where drugs are concerned, but I know that I'm not supposed to smoke pot. The good girl inside me fights with the hungry-for-experience girl as I watch Janet suck deeply on the pipe, then turn red as she holds the smoke in her lungs for as long as possible. By the time she exhales the sweet, heavy cloud, experience has won. I don't feel like such a good girl anymore anyway. There are all kinds of slippery slopes.

I get high and like it. It makes me mellow, an unfamiliar comfort, and life feels more manageable. Nothing bothers me for the duration. When Janet offers me LSD the next night, my good girl is mute, and my hungry-for-experience girl is all in. Janet had already chewed a little blue tab of blotter paper an hour earlier. She sits lotus-style on her bed saying, "Wow, man" and waving her fingers through the air, watching trails of something only she can see.

I don't want to miss out on whatever adventure she's having. I reach for a tab of acid and pop it into my mouth. Ten minutes of chewing later, I begin to feel a neat kind of strange. My glove of skin starts to buzz, and my brain feels soft and porous like I can absorb anything instantaneously. I lift out of my body. Sound, color, and thought become more intense. The next several hours, which could be minutes or days, flash by in plays of color, extraordinary shapes, and fantastical pictures when I close my eyes. Janet and I laugh until tears stream down our faces, then can't remember what was so funny. Wave upon wave of sensation, emotion, and color cascade over me. I've never felt so alive. Everything I see with my vibrating eyes—the bedspread, a picture frame, the carpet, my hands—is its own universe of celestial bodies.

With incredibly dilated pupils, Janet and I see through our own doors of perception, and impressed with our newfound insights, we try to record them but can manage only short bits before we lose the thoughts altogether. As we pick imaginary lint off each other, we feel compelled to write something about "simian," Janet's word, which the next morning, after the hangover, I have to look up in the dictionary. It means "of, relating to, or resembling monkeys or apes."

I know what's coming, but I'm too weak to stop it. Janet makes it clear that she's attracted to me, has certain feelings for me. She's a good-looking girl, but I have neither the attraction nor the feelings. What I have is a crying, almost panicked need for our connection. If I say no, she'll find someone else. We won't be close anymore. So I let us become a couple, a depraved, completely-unfair-to-Janet move on my part. Though I gain the world, I lose my soul to get it.

We are ill matched with no chemistry and now constant fighting. I am so agitatedly uncomfortable being involved with her that I live on edge, irritated by everything. Marijuana doesn't have the same calming effect. We fight about who is supposed to turn off the light, what to do on a Friday night, whether Janis Joplin is a good singer. It doesn't matter. We fight about everything. I'm so miserable, I can't even tell if I'm pretending. Why Janet stays with me can only be explained by her own soul etchings, the unconscious fit of our puzzle pieces. We wrangle along until Christmas.

It's a loaded time of year for me, a season I associate with losing my father and slapping my mother. Skating dangerously close to that fragile trapdoor in my mind, raked with hot and helpless pain, I cut.

It is the Friday night before Christmas break, but I am in no hurry to leave for San Diego. The dorm is practically deserted, and Janet and I are fighting in her room. Like a pinball machine, my brain ricochets between anger at her and frustrated rage at myself. And the shame. Always the shame. Ready to explode, I grab my hair and pull, so hard that tears spring up. Good! I lash out at myself. I'm glad it hurts, I tell myself cruelly. You deserve it, I lash harder, you're a pathetic loser. Look what you'll do for affection.

Janet is all disgust. I've mortally wounded whatever empathy and probably love she ever had for me.

"I'm outta here," she flares and she's gone.

In the silence, I hear my tight, staccato breaths escaping from the iron cage of my chest. Inside my head, the Medusa snakes slither, cold and slick. A seductive thought floats past: There's an X-ACTO knife in Janet's desk.

Slowly I open her top drawer, and there it is, shiny red with a brand-new blade. I drop the knife into my jacket pocket, fingering the grooved hardness of its handle. I push open the heavy door that Janet had slammed on her way out and slip across the hall into my room where I have privacy.

Still ricocheting, I lock the door and take the X-ACTO knife out of my pocket. Someone, maybe the good girl, tries to intervene, but rational thought bounces lightly off my fixation that relief will come only one way: I need to hurt someone—anyone—my mother, my father, Libby, Janet, me.

With the flat edge of the cold blade, I caress the delicate skin on the underside of my left forearm, focusing on a spot halfway between my wrist and elbow. Maybe distress, maybe drugs, maybe a dark spirit fuels my relentless thought: Think how good it would feel to get rid of the shame, Donna. Go on. Do it.

My eyes swim as I steady my shaking hand on my thigh. Ever so carefully, I push the knife into my skin until bright-red blood spurts up.

FIVE

"Life's under no obligation to give us what we expect."
—MARGARET MITCHELL

I saw gently back and forth, trying to hurt myself without hurting myself, an acrobatic feat I will achieve near-perfect mastery of during my life. When the gash is deep enough to pierce the wretchedness, I lift the blade and begin to saw another gash diagonally across the first, an X. The sickening smell of anguish rises with the metallic odor of oozing blood, bringing the first wave of relief. Not enough relief. I lift the blade again and cut another, deeper X into softer, whiter skin.

There is physical pain, but useful pain as it siphons off the pressure in my body. A numbing, almost narcotic swell laps gently at the fire in my brain, slowly, finally, soothing me. Nothing has changed; in fact, I've made things worse, but the momentary release serves its short-sighted purpose. As short-sighted actions are wont to do, this one throws me from the frying pan into the fire.

Back home for Christmas, lingering in bed until the last acceptable minute, I hear my mother laughing. She laughs only with friends, so I know what's happening. She and her best friend are having their weekly kitchen-table coffee and cigarettes before they go shopping. My mother's laugh is hearty and contagious, and an urgent restlessness propels me toward that fleeting ray of sunshine.

They both greet me, the friend, who has known me since birth, quite warmly, my mother pleasantly, always at her best in front of others. They offer me coffee, but this is the bookend of my life where I despise even the smell of coffee, years before I develop an epicurean passion for grinding my own French Roast or Sumatran beans daily, and many years before the bookend where I will renounce it forever. Nonetheless I revel in the offer, included in their moment, and seat myself at the table.

I have left my bedroom so quickly at the sound of my mother's laughter, so driven to reach the sun before it disappears behind the clouds, I've forgotten to pull a long-sleeved shirt over my pajama top. It is only a matter of seconds before the angry red Xs catch the friend's horrified attention.

"What have you done to yourself?" she cries, full of concern.

My arms fly to my chest instinctively, too late to hide anything, and I freeze in a three-way paralysis: angry at myself for being so careless, I can't think of how to go forward; braced toward my mother, I wait for her reaction; touched by the friend's caring, I struggle to hold the dam against a surging longing for more of her kindness.

One beat goes by. Two beats.

Then my mother, with the forced brightness that telegraphs her fragility, chirps, "Oh, just crazy things kids do at college."

She stands up.

"We should get going, don't you think? We'll miss all the bargains."

The friend and I look at each other. So much is said in that look. I want to matter. She wants to help me. But we both know we can't. We have to take care of my mother. Slowly, the friend also pushes back her chair.

"Well, honey," she says softly, "I hope next semester is a really good one."

They leave. I go back to bed. None of us ever mentions it again.

Of all the ways my mother's limitations make her hurt me, this one will linger longer and sadder than any other. She sees me drowning and walks by. Yet even for this, I will finally attain, long after my mother has died, a bittersweet tenderness for her. After the friction of my mother's mortal life has ebbed, I will wish to reach back and comfort the woman who loved me but couldn't love me. And in my compassion for her, I will find compassion for the nineteen-year-old at that kitchen table who wants so badly to feel the sun, who wants so badly to matter.

I stumble blindly back to Berkeley, back to Janet.

I know I need help. I think I know where to get it. Dr. Fader had offered me nothing of value, but he did lay down a template. I think I need to talk to someone about what's going on, but this time, I want to talk to someone who won't judge me for being with a woman. I want the Pacific Center on Telegraph Avenue, a sliding-scale counseling center for lesbians and gays. I see my counselor, a thirty-something intern, on Wednesdays between English 1B and Folklore.

She is nondescript in her loose T-shirts and baggy pants but notable for the metalwork in her mouth, which is held in place by clear rubber bands that expand and contract as she speaks and which give her a pronounced lisp. During our sessions, she strokes her long brown hair, braided into one plait and pulled over her shoulder.

It is a relief to unburden myself about Libby and to talk to someone, finally, about the Xs. After the stupid carelessness at my mother's, I never leave my arms uncovered, and tell Janet I sprained my wrist to explain the Ace bandage. The intern is reassuring about Libby and solicitous about the Xs. When I begin to express my turmoil at being involved with Janet when I really want to be with men, the intern is suddenly less receptive.

"Leth talk about denial."

She strokes her braid.

"What do you mean denial?" I frown.

"We live in a culture where we're taught to shuppreth homothexual urgeth."

She strokes more rapidly as she warms to her subject.

"Ath women, it can be frightening to be our authentic thelvth when we are perthecuted and harathed for loving women. We try to convinth ourthelvth that we are really heterothexual."

Stroke, stroke, stroke.

"What if my authentic self wants to be with men?" I ask, feeling a bit like a scuba diver searching for air bubbles to find the surface.

"Unlikely, given your hithory."

Stroke, stroke, stroke.

"It doesn't feel right for me to be with women," I protest. "I think about men all the time. I want a boyfriend!"

She stops stroking.

"I'm afraid our time ith up for today."

I go back to the braid-stroking intern a few more times, afraid to be honest that she isn't helping anymore. I pretend to make the adjustment to normative lesbianism, thank her, and discontinue the relationship.

Pretending works. That's why I do it. No one is mad at me, no one judges me, I'm safe. It also deadens whatever feelings I have left, which makes it possible to continue with Janet another year, and move with her into a house in the Berkeley hills that we share with three other lesbian couples from the dorm. They are still my only friends.

I daydream about boys as I ride my blue Yamaha moped, given to me by my financially generous mother, back and forth to campus.

UC Berkeley becomes my escape and my oasis, an invigorating intellectual world where no pretending is necessary. I am made for Cal or Cal is made for me, a smorgasbord of perceptions, concepts, theories, and ideas. And deep analysis and discussion. I am in heaven. I never hear the words, "You think too much" or "Lighten up," and the freedom opens up before me like a limitless highway. It is exactly what I need, like a race car needs to go full throttle. My mind is finally able to rev.

So far my life has existed without patterns, without a larger context. Suddenly concepts like imperialism, racism, and homophobia—the stuff of breath at Berkeley—open my mind to a worldview I didn't know existed. There is a ringing truth in all of them that grounds me. Where I have been unable to connect interpersonally, I now connect ideologically, breadth if not depth. It is the first time since Libby that I feel fully engaged.

Little more than a decade after police shot demonstrators protesting the university's plans for a parking lot, and the National Guard had to be called in, there are few places as radical as Berkeley. I love it. It could not be more different from the culture and worldview in which I was raised. That may or may not be part of the allure. As a man thinketh, so is he. I dive into an ocean of uncharted territory that allows me to become a new person. When I encounter the idea of sexism in Kate Millett's Sexual Politics, the next before and after, it literally changes my life. I will never see anything the same way again.

The next three years are a cultural, educational, ideological feast I will never regret. I will imprint so strongly the values of Berkeley—like the first impression in a pair of Birkenstocks—that decades later, in a completely different and much more traditional life, I will be incapable of entirely suppressing a shudder at the mention of certain conservative public figures or a certain political party.

The feast is a sumptuous ride of all five senses. Anti-apartheid rallies, reggae music, Buddhism, cuisine from every corner of the world, and a debate between two ex-cons: G. Gordon Liddy, Watergate burglar, and Timothy Leary, a man Richard Nixon once called "the most dangerous man in America."[1] The San Francisco Gay Freedom Day Parade is history in the making; only twelve years old, it is one of the first three, along with Chicago and New York, in the country. As many times as I attend the parade, nothing is more thrilling than the annual lead-off contingent, block after block of topless, self-proclaimed "Dykes on Bikes"—anything from Harleys to mopeds—with their similarly topless girlfriends perched on back.

Although I hate the label, I suppose I am bisexual, capable of attraction to either gender. I don't like the sound of it, so indiscriminate and devoid of nuance, although I will wear it like a badge of honor when it suits me later with the straight men turned on by such things. I will prefer to say, "I've been with women." It sounds more personal, more like who I really am, a woman who wants to be with men but who is not captured entirely by that definition, a woman who possesses what will be a lifelong bond and allegiance to the nonheterosexual world. My experiences make me who I am, and I cannot leave myself behind no matter what future choices I may make.

---

[1] Laura Mansnerus, "Timothy Leary, Pied Piper of Psychedelic 60s, Dies at 75," *New York Times*, June 1, 1996.

Ambivalent as I am about my relationship with Janet, I nonetheless join with her and all the girls we know in taking a Gay Studies class, the twelfth annual offering of a course that UC Berkeley pioneered in 1970. I have, of course, never heard of the 1969 Stonewall riots in Greenwich Village, New York, considered to be the watershed event that launched the gay rights movement. In the state that made legal history in 1950 by being first in the nation to reduce the crime of sodomy to a misdemeanor, regular police raids on gay bars in New York City continued, including the Stonewall Inn, one of the few establishments receptive to homosexuals.

The sixties were a time of sexual liberation on all fronts, and in an increasingly permissive culture, the gay community grew weary of continued police targeting. Shortly after 3:00 a.m. on June 28, during yet another police raid, Stonewall patrons fought back, a spontaneous and violent uprising quelled only by New York riot police. Within a year, UC Berkeley offered the first undergraduate Gay Studies class in the country, and New York, Chicago, and San Francisco launched their Gay Freedom Day Parades.

The Stonewall riots are, to me, as righteous, and as heartbreaking, as any Civil Rights demonstrations against white oppression. Learning about them and the identities, lives, history, and perceptions of people like me, solidifies both my self-acceptance and my loyalty to the group. I put off what I know is the inevitable end to my relationship with Janet and focus on school.

I decide to become a psychopharmacologist and study the effect of drugs on the mind. My goal is to enter the University of the Pacific as a pharmacy graduate student, which means organic chemistry as an undergrad. I have a B+ in the class—one of my proudest accomplishments—the day I blow up the lab.

I am dressed like everyone else in a white lab coat and plexiglass safety goggles. We are boiling nitric acid. The fumes are so noxious that each beaker is vented to the hood above by plastic tubing inserted into the beaker's black rubber stopper, and my beaker, unlike everyone else's, is turning dark and cloudy. I call over the TA, a graduate student working under the professor's purview.

What happens next will replay in my mind a hundred times. Looking back it will seem so obvious that the beaker is failing to vent properly, that the resulting black smoke indicates an extreme amount of pressure. I will never understand why, because the mistake will also seem obvious in hindsight, but the TA's first move is to pop the black rubber stopper from the top of my beaker.

A geyser of nitric acid explodes upward.

Another accident of birth, or gift from God, is perfect timing. I always seem to be at the right place at the right time. I am so perfectly placed in relation to the geyser that its travel back through gravity misses me entirely. It does not, however, miss the TA. The highly corrosive acid penetrates his clothes even more easily than it sizzles through the black laminate table's top layer. He runs to the shower in the corner of the room, and I gape, horrified, as he struggles to undo his belt then strip off his shirt and pants.

I don't remember the shower being part of our safety instruction. Maybe I wasn't paying attention or maybe undergraduates are not expected to do the advanced kind of work that can cause explosions. In either case, I realize now with perfect clarity that this is why the shower is here. It probably saves his life.

I drop the class the next day.

The professor, a German I have seen only from great distance in the massive lecture hall, attempts to talk me out of it, but I am not persuadable. Organic chemistry, and therefore pharmacy, is not for me. I hurriedly switch to psychology, a major that allows me to focus on the mind without losing my fingers.

Simultaneously, my situation with Janet reaches intolerable limits, one explosion prompting another bursting of sorts. I finally tell her that I have to try being with men.

I tell her, and I mean it at the time, "I wish I had met you five years from now, so that I could already have tried being with men, and then I could be with you."

She doesn't take it well.

The other lesbians in the house are equally jolted. I overhear two of them talking about me.

"What does she think she is, straight or something?" I hear one say.

My time in the female nurturing nest is over. I am unceremoniously pushed out.

SIX

*"I'll try anything once, twice if I like it,
three times to make sure."*
—MAE WEST

My free fall from the nest is cushioned by the fading warmth of its nurturing, the very fortification that gave me the strength to break free. Alone in the world of men—uncharted territory, no markers, no boundaries—drugs and alcohol keep me company.

I want a man to fall madly in love with me, to rescue me from the loneliness that alcohol, especially, keeps at bay. What I cannot keep at bay, and what will appear not so magically in every new pas de deux, are the ever-deepening soul etchings I bring with me. Lack of feeling is the hallmark and double-edged sword of my etchings, the strength that allows me to survive any situation, the weakness that skews my intuitive compass.

My new roommate, a veteran of the dorm, is a Marlboro-smoking, tequila-drinking Korean with a gold pinky ring. Our apartment is west of campus in "the flats," Berkeley-speak for the wrong side of the tracks. Next door to us a barefoot, dreadlocked Rastafarian smokes ganja outside his open door all day. His woman, a blonde with her own impressive set of dreadlocks, traipses in and out with their passel of light-eyed, dreadlocked kids. Next to the Rasta family are two political-science majors, juniors at Cal. Simon, the tall one, is the first to suggest himself as a possibility, the first opening in my new life where I control what happens to me, where I matter.

"Hey," he nods as we pass on the landing, he on his way up, me on my way down.

I manipulate my arrivals and departures to coincide with what I hope will be his, always sure to shine like the sun every time our paths cross. Within a few days, I get results. He stops this time when he sees me coming down.

"Hi there," he grins. "I'm Simon. You're Donna, right?"

I flush with pleasure. This is going even better than I hoped.

"How do you know my name?"

"My roommate met your roommate the other day and says we should double date."

"Great!" I say, my heart skidding to a stop when he says, "But I don't know . . . I've never dated a smoker before."

A quick scan of his face tells me he's mostly teasing.

"Then we're even," I shrug, nonchalant. "I've never dated a man before."

Not exactly true if I count the French guy, but in my mind, this is a clean slate.

His eyes brighten considerably. We agree that fondue and a movie on Saturday works.

Immediately I morph into his perfect woman, definitely not a smoker. I still smoke furiously during the day, but in the evening, I take another shower complete with shampoo and blow-dry, in case he drops by. I sit by the door, waiting. I can make this happen.

I am everything I think Simon wants me to be—charmed by his jokes and his stamp collection—but still he breaks it off when he meets, as he puts it, the love of his life, a nice Jewish girl. After I shake off the bucket of cold water, I recalibrate. I must not be sexy enough, I decide, which must mean less clothing and more alcohol.

One night of heavy drinking later, Dominic—"Nick the Prick" I will think of him for sneaking out afterward in the middle of the night—drives me home in his black Porsche. Between French guy, Simon, and Dominic, I am sexually cosmopolitan—semi-shamed, semi-proud of my jaded status. I have proof that I'm attractive to men, that I matter. It's heady and powerful. I like how men react to my brazenness, their eyes glittering like I am Christmas morning, an effect buoyantly feminizing in the moment, wrenchingly indiscriminate in retrospect.

I strut from Dominic to Jeff to David to Ron, the only pattern being a high proportion of Jewish men and what I will recognize far too late is a wanton disregard for my value on either side. Jewish men shift my view of myself, the first hint that I have a certain kind of appeal to a certain kind of man from a certain kind of culture that embraces strong, intellectual women. My intensity, which has always seemed overpowering in my own white-bread culture of surfer dudes and Presbyterians, is suddenly an asset.

I have dodged a bullet, no longer trapped in the cul-de-sac of women, triumphant in my new sexuality, in control of my future. I savor my sexual effect on each new man and secretly pride myself on my power, on being that kind of girl. Like a girl, I will remember their names for the rest of my life; I will later doubt that any of them remember mine.

Also something of a triumph, school is, post–organic chemistry, going smoothly. Psychology comes easily to me, and when I work with mentally unstable people outside my own family for the first time, I discover I have a certain talent for it. With other psych majors, I drive to Napa State Mental Hospital once a week, forty minutes northeast of Berkeley through world-famous wine country. The four-story, five-hundred-bed, Gothic building has been around for more than a hundred years, and my group is only the latest in a long line of UC Berkeley volunteers to host games and social activities for the chronic schizophrenics.

I feel oddly comfortable with their rocking, their outbursts, their invasion of personal space, and the tongue thrusting symptomatic of long-term antipsychotic medication. The appropriate ones are more disconcerting, and I wonder what they've done to land on a locked unit. One in particular catches my attention, a smoldering woman with an American Indian look, about my age, in a blue-and-white bandana. Her clothing, her haircut, and the way she carries herself all suggest lesbian, and I approach her to start the dance of conversation, ear tuned to certain phrasing that will confirm my suspicion. She starts first.

"Hey how'ya doin'? Got a cigarette?"

She is extremely attractive in a butch sort of way with pale green eyes. I study them, wondering if schizophrenia is something that shows in the pupils since I can't see any evidence of it in her behavior.

"No, sorry, they don't allow us to bring personal items onto the unit," I tell her. "I'm Donna. It's nice to meet you."

"Carla," she declares.

"We,"—I gesture to the other volunteers—"have some games if you're interested."

"Nah," she says, "I really need to find a smoke."

My own pack and a half a day habit understands.

"Well, let me know if you change your mind."

A minute later, she's back with a lit cigarette in the corner of her mouth and an extra behind her ear.

"My girlfriend used to send me money, but we broke up. Now I have to bum."

And there it is. She made it easy for me.

"So you had a girlfriend?" I follow up. "I used to, but we broke up, too."

Carla eyes me approvingly, exactly the response I was hoping for, a tug on the bruised ache I feel for my old friends. I miss connecting with women. I miss it so much that Carla becomes more important to me than she should, and I rely on her too heavily for friendship, a diagnosed schizophrenic on a locked unit I see once a week.

Reaching for more, beyond the pale of standard volunteer behavior, I bring in precious childhood photos to show her. It is one thing to share the pictures, another to leave them behind, which I do in a misguided attempt to feel closer to her. It is a huge mistake. One week she and my pictures are there, the next she is discharged home to Florida, and I have no idea where my pictures have gone. Not that it matters in the grand scheme of things, but they are the cutest pictures of me ever taken, the best evidence that my parents loved me. They tether me to what is good about my family, and their loss burns sharply.

I refocus myself on things I can control. Through another psych major, I meet Zeke, the next notch along my conveyer belt of men, a New York Jew in a black leather jacket. He is an even blend of culture and counterculture, mainstream enough to finish college, rebellious enough to question everything. He calls women "broads," a term I like, something I aspire to be, a woman who is so sexually powerful that she needs nothing from men, not even respect.

The only chemistry between us is the fleeting kind from new attention, but it doesn't matter. I won't realize for years, not until it finally happens, that I've never felt real chemistry. The sex is means to an end, reassurance continuously renewed that I am attractive to men, that I matter. It isn't meant to be personal.

"Hey, Zeke, want to have some fun for the summer?"

Brazenness is my MO. I have nothing to lose and don't really care what the answer will be even though it's fairly predictable. Zeke is no dummy. I use the bisexual card with him, a plus, which he in turn shares—a mistake—with his father, the man who taught Zeke everything he knows about broads.

Other friends have moved on at the end of school, and we find ourselves in need of companionship as well as sex. We listen to Stevie Ray Vaughan, play backgammon, and ride Zeke's Yamaha motorcycle up into the hills after which he carefully pats the brownish-red poof of curls on the top of his head back into place. We smoke cigarettes and pot, do Ecstasy, magic mushrooms, MDM, and MDA. Our friendship is cemented the day we drop acid on the stone steps of the Berkeley Theological Union.

Zeke is all red—mustache, goatee, poof of curls, and red swim trunks with a pink dress shirt rolled up at the sleeves and open at the neck to show his gold ram's horn necklace. It is late summer, and we have the place to ourselves. Lounging and talking for hours, it becomes a shining memory undimmed by anything that follows.

Whether it's the energy of the sun, the vibrancy of our laughter, or the clarity of the air, I need Zeke to know, "I will never forget this moment," and I never do.

We connect, and although the spark is all intellect, no emotion, it reaches deeper than any other connection I've known. I have never been friends with a man, but something about Zeke makes me trust him. We communicate in the same careful, almost over-precise locution. He turns out to be a deep thinker and can take anyone at Trivial Pursuit. I'm impressed that he owns a reproduction of Magritte's Raining Men and a Chemiakin lithograph. I feel at home with Zeke, and that, along with the fact that he sticks around longer than a few weeks, makes him The One.

In his apartment, listening to Bob Marley on a bright afternoon, I blurt out, "I love you."

Zeke is kind.

"Wow," he says sincerely, "I can't honestly say I feel the same way, but I'm really flattered."

"That's cool, no problem," I answer, going right back to the music, only momentarily chagrined.

I really don't expect much. At least he doesn't leave.

In a matter of days, whether flattery wears him down, or whether the put-together parts of me intrigue him, Zeke comes back with, "I feel the same way now."

My reaction is twofold: a deep surge of satisfaction—I really do matter—and a whoosh backward, my sudden disinterest in sex exactly balancing the new level of closeness between us. Emotional distance, my need for it unconscious and pernicious, is the constant. Only because Zeke has his own reasons for connection without emotion—his "secret" he will call it when he finally breaks down after years of marriage—does he stay. Over the next nine years, we will have sex maybe a hundred times, and all but a handful of those times, we will both be wasted. We are in this as in every other way, perfect for each other, at least on paper.

We look at life the same way and make fun of the same things, like "the Mormon Monstrosity," Oakland's LDS temple. We're the same age, both of us are Berkeley grads, neither of us is religious, neither of us wants children, and both of us care about helping people. After a while, I can't imagine ever being without him, and, profoundly feminist since Kate Millett, I advance.

"Hey, I was thinking . . . I want to spend the rest of my life with you."

I watch for his reaction, not really expecting to matter enough, not surprised that he backs away again, kindly because he is kind.

"I can't honestly say I feel the same way," he squeezes my hand, "but I'm really flattered."

Another moment of chagrin, but the overwhelming sense I have is safety. What I don't understand about soul etchings, despite my bachelor's in psychology, is how right it feels when they find their perfect fit, how comfortable, how familiar, how safe. Never mind whether the fit is healthy.

For Zeke's part, it is as much flattery as our interlocking fingerprints that brings him back a few days later with, "I feel the same way now."

Life experience yet to happen will temper my feminism with a healthy respect for the innate differences between men and women. I will never deny a woman's right to pursue a man, but I will learn through rueful experience that it often backfires. Flattery can bring a man to the dance, but if he isn't sufficiently motivated to pursue in the first place, he may not stay for the whole ball.

For now we are a couple, each of us twenty-two, finished with our education, ready to play grown up. We move in together. Devoid of parental guidance on sex, living together, or marriage, I lean on my own understanding to make this decision, which, without values isn't really a decision at all but simply the next step. Years later, my mother will remark that my sister called our moving in together "ruining" my life.

Surprised, I will ask my mother, "Did you think I was ruining my life, too?"

"Yes," she will answer simply.

"Then why didn't you say something?" I will demand, but she will have no answer.

It will remind me of her oft-repeated remark, said in jest, that I raised myself. Sitting atop the ash heap of my life, I will feel all of the burden and none of the amusement.

In truth, moving in together can't ruin my life because my relationship with Zeke is already off track, not that my skewed intuitive compass sends up any warnings. It's tricky because he's such a great person—I've never liked or respected anyone more. As friends we are solid, but as lovers, there's that elephant in the room.

Doubling down, we move into a studio apartment in North Oakland, a light-filled space with dark hardwood floors and floor-to-ceiling windows, all of which are disappointingly north facing. I realize too late that sunlight, the only reliable source of warmth in my life, never enters a north-facing window. It is agitating, almost painful, to see and not be able to feel the embrace I know is there.

On the first day in our new home, Zeke urinates out the kitchen window onto the neighbors' driveway below.

Somehow this isn't the fantasy I've nurtured of being with a man. Coming from our second-floor apartment, it is a long stream and, by the time it hits the ground, quite loud, spattering back up against the building. I can't believe—and will never completely understand—what's happening. I've assumed that being with a man is the answer to everything, and I'm unprepared for such a shock.

"Zeke!" I screech. "What are you doing?"

"What?" He sounds annoyed. "I had to go."

He shakes himself, retreats inside, zips up, and closes the window.

I want to hide under a rock. Two expressions—one French, one English—jostle each other in my mind. "You never get a second chance to make a first impression" makes me want to scream that I can't take back peeing out the window as the first impression we make on our new neighbors. "Il pleut comme vache qui pisse," the French version of "It's raining cats and dogs"— only their idiom, more to the point, "It's raining like cow piss"—makes me want to scratch Zeke's eyes out. Embarrassment and utter lack of control bring out the fury in me.

"Are you out of your mind?" I yell. "You can't pee out a kitchen window! What is wrong with you?"

"All right, all right, cool your jets!" he lashes back, and the fight is on.

It is not the first, not even close to the last, the arguments between us so many and so fierce that Zeke will tell me toward the end, "I want someone with the volume turned down next time."

The conflict serves its purpose, however, and the disturbing truth of what just happened is subsumed under my anger. It saves me the trouble of having to pretend I don't see red flags. I am entirely consumed by how mortified I am that someone might recognize me as the urinator's girlfriend. It's like a religion this being with a man and with Zeke in particular. No matter what assaults my senses, I rationalize it away. Zeke and I are together; everything else is secondary.

We proceed to set up house under a cloud.

SEVEN

*"The seeker embarks on a journey to find what he wants
and discovers, along the way, what he needs."*
—WALLY LAMB
The Hour I First Believed

The wheel of fortune spins us into our first real jobs after graduation. I apply as the evening supervisor of a rehabilitation center, a place with the word "recovery" in its name, which I assume means alcohol and drug recovery, mostly wishful projection on my part. When I get a call from a head injury recovery center, my momentary surprise is replaced with why not? Free as I am in this magical time of life to go wherever the wheel spins, I throw a dart at health care. Zeke also works in health care, a residential facility for emotionally disturbed adolescents. His boss is a pagan.

Once upon a time, "pagan" would have been an off-putting word to me, suggestive of things dark and primitive, most decidedly ignorant. Five years in Berkeley has softened my lens

on the word. I have long since rejected the white, patriarchal Jesus of my upbringing, not that he was much of a
central figure in the way we worshipped, either in church
as I recall or at home where we didn't worship at all. The
only time we ever bowed our heads was at Thanksgiving
and then only, it seemed to me, to give my mother center
stage as The One Who Prayed. I have never had a personal
relationship with any deity, and it is no loss to jettison
Presbyterianism for something a lot more tangible like tarot
cards and astrology charts.

Zeke's boss, Bebi, is Jewish, that's how she and Zeke first connect. When she and her husband buy a house in the Piedmont
area of Oakland, we are first in line to rent their one-bedroom
shoe box at the top of the Oakland hills, a not-fabulous house
but a more-than-fabulous location.

Power lines carve a sweeping overlook of the entire Bay
Area, one of the world's most magnificent views that we enjoy
from our seats on the guardrail. San Francisco, known locally
as Oz, rises to greet the Bay Bridge, which curves gracefully
from Oakland through Yerba Buena Island. On crystal-clear
days washed clean by rain, the Golden Gate Bridge is a thing
of red beauty against a blue jewel, half sky, half ocean.

Around a narrow, dead-end curve, our house perches on a
nearly vertical hillside canopied in giant Eucalyptus trees. A
deck runs the length of the house, doubling its entire width to
thirty feet. In summer's sweltering heat, when the air is dead
still, we sleep on the deck's futon bed under our menthol sky,
grateful for any stirring of leaves.

On the brown doorframe of our brown shoe box, Zeke hangs a mezuzah to protect us, a cultural tradition from a religion he has never practiced, much to the sorrow of his grandmother who derides me as a shiksa. Neither of us has any sympathy for her. My religious sentiments have yet to be awakened; Bebi will light that torch momentarily.

She is a green-eyed stunner, yoga fit, with straight brown hair that hangs to her shoulders. Her two front teeth are dead and brown, separated by a sizable gap, but it only adds to her exoticness. I will wonder, as she introduces me to the delights of matriarchal religion, if it is some statement against the patriarchy that she has never had them fixed. We fall into an easy friendship during the house handover.

Bebi is who I want to be when I grow up: beautiful, professionally successful, married, a homeowner. Without a mother bond in my life, I'm drawn to women role models like a moth to flame, all sponge as she takes me on a tour of her new house. We start with her altar, a low table covered in crystals, orange candles burning in tall glass jars, and an Egyptian-looking figurine, breasts bared, clutching writhing snakes in both fists above her head.

Bebi lights a bundle of herbs tied with string. She is, she tells me, cleansing the sacred space with sage. I watch the smoking embers as she waves them in slow, Thanksgiving-smelling circles, then taps them out in the basin of a shiny abalone shell. When she produces a round deck of cards from a black velvet bag, I am riveted.

The cards, "tarot" Bebi calls them as she lays them out, display vivid, unusual images: a woman draped in leopard skin stretched out on the ground in front of a mirror; a male religious figure with breasts; a female body of stars arcing across the sky above a chariot; a naked woman, upside down, dark hair flowing to the ground, hanging from a tree by her ankle. Their shape is round, Bebi says, because patriarchy is square, and the Goddess is matriarchal, cyclical like the moon. She fingers the cards lovingly, and I feel pulled to touch them myself, to feel their smooth surfaces, delve into their symbols.

Bebi looks at me.

"There was a time when everyone worshipped the Goddess and nature. The male-dominated church with its father and son gods was a much later development."

I nod. A vision of connection with women, with female gods, opens in my mind. I am immediately receptive, drawn toward the feminine bonds I want so badly.

"You know what witches are?" Bebi asks in a low tone.

I wince inwardly and shake my head. Open-minded I am, but "witch" is a scary word, and Bebi seems about to bring me closer to that world.

"Wise women!" she hoots. "That's where the word 'Wiccan' comes from, 'wise ones.' They were wise women who healed with herbs and esoteric knowledge."

I nod again—witches are just wise women—and slip over another line, following Bebi to the end of this road, wherever it goes.

"Witch hunts," she goes on, "were male doctors trying to get women out of the healing business—too much competition!"

Bebi snorts, and I bristle at the audacity of those men, those insecure, threatened, patriarchal men who wanted all the power for themselves.

"They made it illegal for anyone but doctors to heal," she declares, "and only men could be doctors. Killed a lot of knowledge in the process."

I think about this while she lays out more cards. In a few words, Bebi has illuminated hundreds if not thousands of years of history for me. So much of it clicks into place, like parts of a picture emerging when enough puzzle pieces are joined together. My world is all of a sudden more understandable, more manageable, and I feel a surge go through me.

"I get it," I say, "I . . . get . . . it."

Bebi is watching me, watching the light come on.

"That's where tarot cards come from. They keep the Ancient Wisdom alive."

She hands me a card with a beautiful, braided young woman in a pool of water ringed with plants and flowers. I notice the roman numerals for seventeen at the top and the word "Star" at the bottom.

"How do you feel when you look at The Star card?" Bebi asks.

I study the lavender background, the bird in the sky, the woman's lovely, upturned face, and ask myself the same question.

"I don't know."

I run my fingers over the image, feeling its slippery coolness under my hand, trying to feel its energy.

"Calm, maybe?"

"Exactly!"

She smiles, pleased.

"That's exactly right. The Star card is about calm after the storm . . . refreshment . . . cleansing . . . and nobody needed to tell you that. That's the power of these images!"

Bebi puts a triumphant point on it.

"That's the power of women!"

"Hmmm." I assimilate.

I look back at the card. I see it. I feel it. It will turn out to be one of my favorite cards.

Bebi goes on.

"Each card has a tiny piece of the Ancient Wisdom, and the whole deck is Truth. The twenty-two named cards, like this one," she taps the card in my hand, "are like facets on a diamond, and each facet of truth reveals an aspect of Ancient Wisdom."

"Hmmm," I say again.

I pick up the other cards she's laid out and examine each one. Woman draped in leopard skin is number three, The Empress. Sky woman is number seven, The Chariot. Naked woman hanging from tree is number twelve, The Hanged One. Guy with breasts is number five, The Hierophant.

"What's a hierophant?" I ask.

"It means 'someone who reveals sacred things.' It's from the Greek. In tarot it stands for a teacher, or a priest, or some other kind of spiritual authority figure."

"So why does he have breasts?" is my obvious question.

"Because male religious figures steal power from women. Women have to submit to men's authority in the patriarchal church. They're cut off from their organic connection to the beauty in nature, and the male authority makes himself their only source of religious information."

"Hmmm."

That's a lot to digest, but Bebi is so beautiful, so smart, so successful. I want to be like her, want to be a part of her world that turns on the power of women. I consider how unfair it is that women can't be priests in the Catholic Church. Each new bit of Bebi's teaching slides down a little bit easier than the one before.

Bebi's voice rises, her admiration evident.

"The Wise Ones were smart. They knew no one would care about simple playing cards, and the Wisdom would pass right under the religious authorities' noses. Did you know that the playing cards we use today are actually tarot cards?"

I blink.

"What?"

In fifth grade, Mrs. Sewall let the kids who finished work early play gin rummy. I played a lot of gin rummy that year.

"Mmm hmm. Our playing cards today are all the minor tarot cards. They took out all the named cards but one."

Bebi holds up a card that is number zero, The Fool.

"Look familiar?"

She tilts her head at me while I register the image.

"It's The Joker!" I realize with a jolt.

"Right again," she grins. "Think about it, what would have been the most powerful thing that primitive humans ever witnessed?"

Her gray-green eyes grip me, and I try to imagine what it might be.

"Women giving birth!" Bebi laughs. "They saw life coming out of women's bodies. Don't you think that would have made them worship women? It did! That's how we got the Goddess!"

"Okay," I nod, a mental slide show progressing through my head.

"It was only when men realized they had a part in procreation that they took over! That's how we got male gods."

Bebi sits back, lesson delivered.

I sit back, lesson absorbed.

She leans forward again.

"Do you know why the number thirteen is considered unlucky? Because it's the number of the Goddess!"

I wrinkle my forehead.

"The Goddess has a number?"

"Yes! The same number as moons in a year. Thirteen. Thirteen lunar months a year. Thirteen is the number of the female."

Bebi tries it several ways until I react.

"Oh."

"That's why thirteen is an unlucky number in a patriarchal society."

"Ohhh."

"Twelve is the number of patriarchy. The male god is associated with the sun. That's where the name "son" of god comes from. There are twelve solar months in a year, and that's why there were twelve apostles."

I've heard enough. I'm ready to dive into this world ruled by goddesses.

"Where can I get a deck like this?"

Bebi chuckles.

"Gaia. In Berkeley. You can get everything you need there."

Gaia is a metaphysical world unto itself, a universe of magic wands, pagan books and manuals, incense, drums, crystals, Goddess figurines, sage sticks, tarot cards, and candles. When I walk in the door, I feel embraced by feminine energy, enticed to fling myself into all of it.

I buy the same tarot cards Bebi has, a beginner's workbook with exercises to learn about the cards, a five-inch long crystal from Brazil, some candles, a sage stick, and an abalone shell.

I start my library with two books the clerk says I have to have: The Encyclopedia of Women's Secrets, a three-inch thick book of all things pagan, and The Holy Book of Women's Mysteries, a book of spells by the Bay Area's most famous witch, Z Budapest.

Still unsettled by the idea of witchcraft, I feel a squeezing between my ribs when I read Z's spell for hexing a rapist. Somewhere, dimly, I reject the idea of doing harm to others, even rapists, not because I'm so good, but because I believe ninety percent of what we do to others sticks to us. I don't want to get mixed up in hexing. I keep the book though, because I think it lends my library a certain gravitas.

When I announce my intention to worship the Goddess, Zeke, always supportive, builds me my own altar, a square wooden table that sits eight inches off the ground, perfect height for my tarot readings. I paint each leg a different phase of the moon: waxing crescent in a lavender sunset, waxing gibbous in a bright-blue afternoon, luminous full in a jet-black night, waning gibbous in a pale-blue early morning. For the next ten years, I will do a tarot reading at my altar every morning.

There is no question that the cards communicate something otherworldly. Random probability should produce each card with roughly equal frequency, but there are unmistakable patterns, completely different in readings I do for myself than in readings I do for Zeke or other friends. A certain card appears over and over for weeks or months, strangely suited to the present situation, then disappears indefinitely once the situation resolves. Other cards almost never appear.

I think of tarot as a mirror. Other people may use the cards to tell fortunes, but I always interpret them as showing a life situation in pictures, a way to speak to the deeper, nonrational parts of the mind and access creative problem solving. Clarity is the mother of choice.

I look for connection, connection, always connection, and tarot connects to numerology, astrology, magic, alchemy, Kabbalah, and chakras, even Judaism. I explore them all. I love that understanding the meaning of a number, say the protection and stability of the number four, gives more meaning to the number-four tarot card, The Emperor. Studying astrological signs like Leo, The Lion, helps me understand The Strength card, a woman opening a lion's mouth. All of it gives me a soothing sense of control, a world I can manage, a world that makes sense in a gentle, beautiful way, a world of women.

I want the purpose of a life that follows the cycle of the moon. I want the intellectual charge of a worldview that connects everything back to the Goddess. I want the sense of safety that flows from connecting to a power larger than myself, specifically a mother power.

What I don't want is to be like other people I see in the pagan world, people in flowing robes and patchouli oil, free spirits who disdain mainstream culture and make me uneasy. I might break rules, but I orient myself always in relation to them. I find a fair degree of safety in my allegiance to institutional authority, and I don't want to leave that world; I simply want to bring a little paganism into it. I want what Bebi has. Like her I want to live a life of makeup, tailored clothing, and capitalism, a life that happens to have a pagan side to it. I just don't want to do it alone.

For the sake of community, I force myself to search the bulletin board at Gaia for opportunities to meet and socialize with other Goddess devotees. My intersection with fate is a brightly labeled business card: Priestess of the Temple of Isis. The priestess is advertising a prosperity celebration in her home, and I decide that's sort of capitalism so I make myself go.

The moment I walk in the door, I want to leave. I regret taking off my shoes. I regret kneeling with the four—only four—other people who have come to be with the priestess. I had been expecting a larger group, a more anonymous situation where I could hang back and observe. We are all in the front row at Priestess Aaliyah's circle, and I am right next to her. I play it cool as she lights a white candle and invokes the Great Goddess.

"Great Mother," she intones, "Mother of Earth, we invoke and call upon you this night to celebrate the fruits of earth which you have so generously provided to us, and to ask your continued blessings of abundance and prosperity."

I'm extremely uncomfortable, self-conscious. This was a bad idea. I work at keeping my face impassive. Everyone is looking at Aaliyah, who has her eyes closed and is starting to sway.

"Mother of Earth, we thank you!"

Her voice pitches up and she falls forward, slapping her palms on the floor, rocking and slapping, rocking and slapping.

"Thank you, Divine Mother, Mother of us all, thank you!"

Her voice is nearly hysterical, and she is sobbing, banging her fists now.

"Thank you Mother, thank you, we are so grateful, so grateful!"

It looks suspiciously like a nervous breakdown. If the room weren't so small, and the group weren't so intimate, I would bolt. But I can't. There is no way to duck out of this, at least not while pretending I'm cool.

Aghast, I watch Priestess Aaliyah open her eyes, look directly at me, and sing-song, "Your turn."

Four pairs of eyes watch for me to commence sobbing. I look down at Aaliyah still on the floor and back up at the expectant eyes in the semicircle around me. There is no way. I have pretended my way through many things, but not full-on gyrating and emoting, not public prostration and weeping. This is not going to happen.

"I am so sorry," I rock back on my heels. "I'm not feeling well. Would you all please excuse me?"

The blood pounds so loudly in my ears, just like at my locker in high school, that I can't hear anything. I shoot out the front door, barely grabbing my shoes. I will push away the anxiety of what they think of me each time it bubbles up, and I will never reach for pagan community again. Connection is vital but not that vital. I can hide who I am, but I can't manufacture parts of myself that don't exist. This isn't me.

I revert to solitary Goddess worship, a space where I can embrace the loveliness of the moon, the beauty of tarot cards, and the connectedness of nature, all from outside of pagan culture. It is me, I learn again, to be alone.

EIGHT

*"Things change . . . things happen . . . things you can't
even imagine when you're young and full of hope."*
—JUDY BLUME

M y relationship with Zeke puts a Band-Aid over a festering wound that's never been cleaned; it calms things down only to have them spurt out in other ways. Someday I will read somewhere, probably in a women's magazine, that if the sex is good, it's twenty percent of the relationship; if it's bad, it's eighty percent. Sex is ninety percent of ours.

I do not want to have it. Not with Zeke. He is attractive, I'm attracted to him intellectually, emotionally, and energetically, and I am also full of red-blooded desire. Just. Not. For. Him. It is so bad, so distasteful to me, that on top of needing to be wasted to make it happen, as soon as it does happen, I flood with relief that I'm off the hook for at least a little while. It is on this sound basis that we discuss marriage.

We are twenty-four, Zeke exactly ninety-two days older than I am, both of us old enough to take that step, neither of us emotionally healthy enough to recognize that we are walking a gangplank to nowhere. In our defense, the ten percent that isn't sex is really pretty good. Pretty good except for all the fighting, which may have something to do with the lack of sex. What will later prove a marked defect in our chemistry—we are the same half of the whole—makes us great friends.

We are so alike—he the more masculine Donna, me the more feminine Zeke—that we are in almost every other way a perfect match. We each lead with our intellect, explain in too much detail, and have a love affair with sarcasm. We are both type As, rising stars on the job, party animals. Neither of us respects Christians or anyone who voted for Reagan, and neither of us notices a lack of romance between us. The decision to marry is all business.

I find a beautiful ring of diamonds and sapphires and buy it for myself as an engagement present. I give Zeke the bill. He then decides that his engagement gift, from me, will be the down payment on a brand new Hyundai. We exchange fifteen hundred dollars, and it is official.

There is no hurry to marry. The most important thing is to time the wedding with the moon. We will wait more than a year for a harvest moon—the full moon closest to the autumnal equinox—to fall on a weekend night, Friday, September 15, 1989. It gives Zeke time to move out.

Fearing the never-had-a-chance-to-do-thats of middle age, or so he tells me, Zeke decides to live on his own for a while, in his own apartment, so that he can settle down happily, again so he says, when we marry. Painted equally broadly among my worldly stripes are naïve ones. I not only help him find an apartment, I help him clean it to within an immaculate inch of its life, no easy feat since Zeke is replacing long-term Vietnamese renters who have cooked in what smells like the same batch of oil for years. Even the metal window frames reek.

The momentous first night of the rest of his life finally arrives, and I drop Zeke off at the BART station. He is supposed to take the train to MacArthur Park, Oakland's version of New York's Central, and walk the rest of the way. He'll be fine. He doesn't look like anyone to mess with, only five feet nine but a solid two hundred pounds.

"Okay," I say, as he gets out, "good luck. Call me when you get there."

"Right," he grins and saunters off with a jaunty wave—we never kiss hello or good-bye—briefcase in hand.

I call him as soon as I get home, excited for him. I call him again fifteen minutes later. And fifteen minutes after that. The FCC approved the first commercial portable cell phone five years earlier, for a mere four thousand dollars, but I haven't even heard about it. I have only my landline phone that I pick up every fifteen minutes for the next several hours, more worried each time Zeke doesn't answer.

I get in my car and drive to the immaculate apartment, but the windows are dark, and Zeke has forgotten to give me a key. I drive home scanning the road on either side, looking for a body or a briefcase. At four in the morning, almost ten hours since I last saw Zeke, my phone rings.

"Zeke! Is that you? Where have you been?"

My words rush out to him, hugging and boxing him at the same time.

"Do you know how long I've been trying to call you?"

Zeke sounds highly pissed.

"I've been trying to call you! Where have you been?" I snap back.

"Jail, okay? I'm in jail," he barks.

"Jail? Why didn't you call me? I've been driving around looking for you!"

Now I'm highly pissed.

"Hey, it's pretty hard to get through when the line's always busy."

Oh. "Why are you in jail?"

"I was walking through the park . . ."

I picture Zeke in his jeans, kelly-green shirt, size XL, and his Guys and Dolls suit jacket from the thrift store with the sleeves rolled up, striding along in his white, scuffed-up Nikes.

". . . and a woman called out to me, 'Hey good lookin', lookin' for a good time?'"

The picture in my head starts to roll like an old-time television set that can't tune the station.

" . . . I didn't even stop walking, just called back over my shoulder, 'What kind of good time?' and the next thing I knew, I was in handcuffs. She was a cop! I got busted by an undercover cop!"

Zeke's voice is full of embarrassment and something else I can't identify.

"How can they do that?" My naïve stripes are indignant. "That's entrapment! That's not right!"

"Well they did. They arrested me for soliciting a prostitute. I need you to bail me out."

Wives see what their husbands want them to see; girlfriends see even less. I can't understand why Zeke's public defender tells him to plead no contest in exchange for a lesser charge of disturbing the peace.

"Why are you pleading no contest when you're not guilty?"

Berkeley education or no, I am baffled by the apparent incongruity of an innocent man admitting to something he didn't do. It will make nauseatingly, blindingly clear, life-altering sense in about three more years.

In the meantime, Zeke's flirtation—as I will come to think of it wryly—with independence is over before it starts. He breaks the lease without ever spending a night there. Somebody gets an outrageously clean apartment. We are back on the expressway to marriage, no detours, no off-ramps.

Now that Zeke is ready to introduce me to his parents, his mistake of sharing my sexual history with them becomes apparent. This is twice Zeke has trapped me in the no-win situation of you never get a second chance to make a first impression. They are gracious in person, but his father follows up with a letter of parental counsel, in short, don't take on the problems of a bisexual.

He compares us to Tristan and Isolde. I know I'm Isolde. I'm not sure if Zeke is Tristan, whom Isolde loves but cannot marry, or if Tristan is my past (and potential future) with women, and Zeke is the poor sot Isolde marries but does not love. We brush it off in either case. Parental wisdom moves us as little as did grandma's religious loyalty.

While we wait for the moon, I make my wedding dress by hand, sewing tiny ivory pearls onto delicate ivory lace by the thousands. I call it my mermaid dress, a sleeveless glove of pearled lace on shimmery satin from neck to knees, and a rippling full flounce of shimmery satin falling the rest of the way to the floor. With three-quarter length satin gloves, it is stunning.

There is something so satisfying about the fine, detailed work of sewing beads the size of a pinhead onto the gossamery filigree. It is a labor of love, long on fantasy, short on reality, although a niggling something at the back of my mind makes me ask Zeke to agree, only half jokingly, that if for any reason we don't go through with the ceremony, he will eat the dress with a knife and a fork. I take the joke on the road, telling it to friends and strangers alike each time the niggling breaks through my fantasy, which extends only as far as the wedding. Our life beyond is a hazy something to manage, much like I manage living with him now. My only focus is the four hours we will party in the Brazil Room in Tilden Park at the top of the Berkeley hills.

In a mixture of denial and compunction, I address the elephant in the room before we marry.

"Zeke?"

My trust in him is absolute, no matter how he responds.

"What if I never want sex again?"

I hold my breath. I really don't want him to leave, but I have to ask. It's only right.

His answer, so bizarre in retrospect, shows the hand-in-glove fit of our soul prints.

"That would be okay," he says, and I've never felt safer.

What should be a red flag on the play is interpreted by me as unconditional love. We see what we want to see.

The night of our wedding settles warm and still over the hills, quiet except for the cars arriving. Zeke's ivory tuxedo matches my dress, but he forgets to take off his tacky black watch. He will be mad at himself for ruining the pictures. We toast champagne with a picture-perfect wedding party that includes my parents and sister, Zeke's parents and siblings, and Janet. All is forgiven, she is happy with her new girlfriend, and we are still good friends. The photographer tells us to hug for the camera, and we break out laughing at the inside joke.

The full moon won't clear the trees until nine, so dancing and more champagne ensue, the live afro-beat band our favorite from the clubs. Once the enormous yellow orb is high in the sky, so bright it could be daylight, we move outside to a clearing under the pines. Thirteen friends—the number of the Goddess—make a circle around us holding red, orange, and yellow candles. The ceremony is pagan all the way, no minister, no vows, just singing and good wishes. The chaplain at Zeke's job had already signed the license so technically, we are already married.

My boss, a sassy Virginia belle known for signing reports with a kiss, sings Van Morrison's "Moondance" a cappella with backup from the occupational therapist, also a friend. Each of the thirteen friends steps forward to offer a wish for our married life together, but I remember only the first one, that each day would be as fresh as the new morning dew. Fresh it will be, and not in a good way, each new drama more unexpected than the last.

Things aren't supposed to change when we get married. We don't mingle our finances, I don't change my name, we don't buy property, and we don't want children. Yet everything changes; we go through the looking glass backward into a whole new existence. When we were living together, we were just Donna and Zeke, but now that we're married, Zeke is a "husband" and I am a "wife." Each of us has a mental archetype for those roles—our parents—and that's who we turn into. In the first six months, Zeke and I each buy and consume our own six-pack of beer on the way home from work every night. Weekends are worse.

Through the alcohol fog and marijuana haze, I read a book on cosmobiological birth control, the completely rational, to my mind at the time, idea that conception is driven by the moon. The book, printed with two missing pages, an oversight I readily overlook, posits that a woman can conceive only during a certain phase of the moon, specifically the phase in which she herself was born.

The moon is my portal to the divine, the source of spiritual meaning in my life, and as such, it elevates our sexual activity to something holy. I have a desire for that if nothing else. I quickly complete my natal astrology chart and determine that the waxing crescent moon—a phase that lasts in the neighborhood of four days a month—is my fertile time. The other twenty-six or so days of the month are worry-free. With Zeke's full agreement, I abandon all other methods of birth control.

Almost immediately, my abdomen feels thick, and a queasy shadow rises with me in the mornings. I am sick, sick, sick, mostly at heart. I have to take three at-home pregnancy tests to believe it is true. The Planned Parenthood test confirms that it is dreadfully, horribly true. Even more dreadful and horrible, I am not pregnant enough to have an abortion. I will have to wait six more weeks, until the fetus is big enough to suck out. This thing inside me feels like an alien I can't get away from, can't get rid of, can't stand. I don't want a baby. At least I don't think so.

Zeke: "It's your decision, Donna, but I don't want a baby."

Girlfriends: "Every woman gets one abortion. You can have your children later."

I don't disagree. I want it out of me, but I draw an entire page of big blue tears in my journal with the words, "Zeke and I made a baby we don't want."

The trapped desperation will haunt me, long after the fetus is gone and I am back at work with a new haircut and a brighter shade of lipstick, and people are telling me how good I look, how there's just something about me. No matter how much conservatism will come to flow in my veins, I will never back away from the conviction that abortion is a highly personal decision for a woman to make prayerfully. But oh, not to know that I have something to pray about, not even to imagine that inside me is something—someone—made of gold, and I throw her away like the trash. I don't know how I know it's a her, but I do. I will think about her every April 22 for the rest of my life.

In the fog and haze of those six weeks before I am set free, I stumble onto another new age idea, a stop-gap measure: psychic abortion. As instructed, I commune directly with the fetus, the only time I feel any openness to her. The communication is too personal, too sacred even for my altar, so I lock myself in the bedroom while Zeke is at work. Leaning back against the bed, I close my eyes to steady my breath, and try to feel her. In the years to come, when my confusion has lifted, I will hope, I will want to believe, that she feels me, too, feels my sincerity amidst the chaos.

"This isn't a good time," I tell her. "Please go away and come back another day when it's more convenient."

She probably knows what I don't: I will never have another chance.

Earthquake, fire, flood, and confession mark the high points of our marriage, not necessarily in that order. On October 17, one month and two days after our moonlit nuptials, a 6.9 earthquake rocks the Bay Area. The shaking, dubbed the World Series Quake and seen live around the world on ABC, starts on a Tuesday at 5:04 p.m. during the warm-up of game three between the Oakland A's and the San Francisco Giants.

Zeke and I, like everybody else on both sides of the bay, have plans to watch the game with friends. Rush hour is empty, most of us already on couches or floors with chips and a beer. I am not

yet a believer in miracles, but a fifty-foot span of the San Francisco–Oakland Bay Bridge collapses and only one person is
killed. Forty-two people lose their lives when the Nimitz Free-
way collapses, but it's a fraction of what it could have been.

This particular Tuesday is my turn to run home and let the
dogs out. Duty completed, I'm chatting with the woman who
lives next door, a community college professor, when the street
starts to lurch. We grab each other's hands, hearts pounding,
eyes fixed on the Eucalyptus trees above us swaying like enormous kelp.

"Oh my god, oh my god, oh my god," she whimpers.

I can't speak. It takes every bit of concentration I have to
get through it. The stress between tectonic plates releases for
fifteen long seconds and then subsides.

A switch flips inside of me, like it always does, a sort of
protective delayed reaction to upsetting events. I don't even
go inside to check on the dogs. Almost blithely, I jump in my
car, hurrying to catch the start of the game. What I see on
television, however, is the footage, shown over and over, of a
lone car plunging off the top deck of the Bay Bridge. Another
switch flips, and I have to get to work, have to get control,
have to protect people. Zeke, my same half, knows exactly
where to find me.

It will take an extra ten days, the World Series on hold while
the city recovers, but the A's eventually sweep the Giants in
four games.

The paper anniversary, our first, is drenched in a flood of my
making. In our shoe box of a house is a shoe box of a kitchen

with a portable dishwasher indeterminate of age but clearly past its better days. The day of our anniversary party, I clamp the black rubber hose to the kitchen faucet, turn on the water full force, and leave for work. When Zeke slogs through the two feet of water after work, reaching to shut off the deluge, he gets a sudden flash, he will tell me and not kindly, of his hands around my neck.

Instead of an anniversary party, there is a party of men who drain the water and rip up the carpet, noting the age of the house and the possibility of asbestos. Instead of the music we planned for our guests, the air is filled with the deafening sound of five humongous, exorbitantly expensive fans that blow for three days. We aren't there to hear them because we have decamped to a dodgy hotel for the duration. Another couple might laugh it off, might consider it a chapter in this adventure called marriage. We don't——a discomfiting hint that something is wrong between us.

Thirty-five days after anniversary two—cotton ironically, a textile that burns into feathery, gray ash—the Oakland hills burst into a conflagration that destroys more than three thousand homes in a single day. Our house, though dry and freshly carpeted, means nothing to us, a tin shack among mansions. We willingly and psychically offer it up to the fire gods if it will spare someone else's home instead.

The next morning, behind yellow police tape, we huddle with other evacuees, silently waiting to trudge through unrecognizable streets marked only by burned-out cars and the solitary remains of chimneys. At the signal, we press forward en masse through smoky air that resembles nuclear winter, the starting pack at a marathon nobody wants to run. Witness to each other's pain, the ghastly intimacy is too much for me, and the switch flips.

What is she crying for, I think, when the young woman ahead of us bursts into tears, my reaction to her heartbreak delayed just long enough so I can cope. Once its meaning breaks through—the rubble she's standing in front of used to be her home—the image of her sobbing, face in her hands, will never leave me.

Survivor's guilt that our house is still standing, that our marijuana plants are safe on the deck, is disconcerting. It feels all wrong. We should be the ones whose lives burned up. I think of the sobbing young woman and push down the thought that Zeke and I don't need our house saved, don't have a life together worth saving.

For almost a year, I pretend things are fine, see what I want to see. Then, because it's not up to me, the curtain lifts, and I see the rest. Zeke tells me his secret.

It will be so obvious in hindsight.

It is late on Sunday afternoon, that in-between time when day slides softly to dusk, and I am restless and lonely. Sunday is the day for family and church, neither of which I want, but I feel the pull of their meaningfulness and my ambivalent place outside it. It is the day we have our worst fights.

"I need to tell you something," Zeke blurts out, his voice wooden.

The image of my dad in my bedroom all those years ago flashes across the screen in my mind.

"Okay," I say, very quietly.

"I've been leading a double life," Zeke says heavily and stops.

Adrenalin shoots through me. This is not going to be good.

"I go to adult bookstores. Prostitutes, too. Since before I met you . . . but . . . since we've been together, too."

Lit with a flash of comprehension, my mind jumps to the night he was arrested. I stare at him, amazed, as it all whooshes together.

"You really were soliciting that night, weren't you?"

I am absolutely stilled by the truth of it, a truth I can feel deep in my bones, a relief actually.

"Yes," Zeke says simply, "but I haven't been with prostitutes since we've been married."

I take it in. It all fits. Why he wanted the apartment, why he pled no contest, why it was okay that I didn't want sex. I feel light, liberated, a little queasy, and strangely curious from my front-row seat.

"What do you do in adult bookstores?"

"I hang out, maybe pick up women. Sometimes there are places in the back you can go."

Zeke unburdens himself, and I watch the tightness ease in his face, watch his shoulders relax.

"But not since we've been married," he adds hastily. "I just hang out there now. That's where I feel comfortable."

I study him for a minute, my husband, this man I don't know. "What's it like being with prostitutes?"

"It's nasty," he shudders.

"Do you kiss them?"

"Hell, no! You get as far away from them as you can and still get the job done."

I picture him with prostitutes, having sex, a porno starring Zeke.

Not a flipped switch this time but a genuinely healthy boundary, maybe my first, asserts itself. I know without a doubt that this is not about me. Pretending things are fine and rejecting him sexually might make me his perfect fit, soul prints and all, but this is about Zeke. I don't and never will take it personally. What I will do is lean in.

In lockstep, my desire for sex increases in proportion to the distance his revelation creates between us, my unconscious goal to maintain the closeness between us, or lack thereof, at a constant level. For the briefest of moments, Zeke's confession spices up our sex life. When our emotional intimacy in turn heats up, I step back to reinject some distance. The more things change, the more they stay the same.

For eight years with me, and who knows how long before that, Zeke has settled for emptiness and shame. The courage it takes for him to tell me his secret sets him free from both. He wants a real marriage now, and he values himself enough to ask for it, delivered in the form of an ultimatum. Either I put up—out—or he's gone. It will take me a year to decide if I can. Zeke waits patiently, as he always has, for me to be ready. I know I love him. I want to be with him. I just need to make myself want sex with him.

Eventually, even I can't pretend it's going to happen. Chemistry isn't made in a test tube. We've known for some time that we don't have it, don't feel that rev for each other, but we've assumed it would grow from respect, regard, and affection. Whether from God or from a process of elimination, I discover the bitterest life lesson to date, a rock-hard truth: if the chemistry isn't there, it isn't there. The insight frees us both.

Faced with the end, we pull back from the brink of divorce. Maybe we can stay married and have sex on the side. For nine years, we've been best friends and life partners, achingly hard to relinquish no matter how we've outgrown each other. In the end, though, the insuppressible hope of happily ever after is too strong. We file for divorce at the Alameda County Courthouse and then go out to breakfast, hearts unbroken, friendship strong.

The truth has set us free, and I intend to follow it from here on out. No more pretending. The truth is, I wanted to make it work with men but I couldn't. Rising like a phoenix from the ashes, I determine to be true to myself. I must be a lesbian after all.

NINE

"I live my life in widening circles that reach out across the world."
—RAINER MARIA RILKE
Rilke's Book of Hours: Love Poems to God

Health care is changing; Cadillac insurance plans are out, HMOs are in. In the tumble, my job disappears, and I jump to the next stone in the river, a license as a nursing home administrator. I am hired as the assistant administrator of a very downtown Oakland facility, of dubious reputation, which will require new ownership and two licensed administrators—myself and my boss—to clean up. I am as white-bread and unprepared for it as I can be.

It is a sea of black. A few white, Filipino, Hispanic, Vietnamese, and Chinese as well but African-American in every way—culture, attitude, style, language. I don't know it, but I am about to totally remake myself. Starting with men.

There is just something about black men. Surfer dudes in San Diego and intellectuals at Berkeley weren't like this. These are real men, or so it seems to my awakened sense of femininity. And they reciprocate my interest. A point will come, much further into my cultural development, when I will appreciate the feelings of black women on the matter.

One sister will say bluntly, "A third of our men are in prison, a third are gay, and a third are with white women—who are we supposed to date?"

Without disputing her numbers, I will decide that for me personally, the right decision is to remove myself from the equation. For now, however, it is the spark that sets everything on fire. I am most definitely not a lesbian. Newly divorced, eyes gleaming, I practically pant after the maintenance crew.

The reverberations of divorce bring other wisdom to the fore, the fundamental kind that's true no matter whom I date. The nursing home is funded primarily by Medi-Cal, and the residents' financial poverty is matched only by their paucity of visitors. I quickly glean the bedrock truth that it doesn't matter how I look, where I live, or what I drive; the only thing that really matters in life is the quality of my relationships.

My heart breaks for the forgotten ones, and I find in myself a wellspring of love for the elderly, not unlike some women feel for babies. Where I am usually irked by vulnerability and dependence, the elderly have earned it. I also like that they're real. There's very little fronting in one's eighties.

One woman, so small she seems dwarfed by her wheelchair, one of the few whose family comes to visit, cuts my heart especially deep. Her white tennis shoes go missing every time her son brings a new pair, which is often since they keep disappearing. It kills me that her addled sweetness never changes; she is as kind and gentle as ever, to everyone. Someone, probably a nurse assistant who feeds or bathes her, those most intimate of duties, probably at a time when the building is most deserted, is stealing her shoes. I feel fiercely protective of her. Cleaning up the building means, in part, clamping down on this and other rampant theft. My boss and I go about it in very different ways.

He is by far the smarter one, the shining star brought in by corporate to turn the place around. He is charismatic, high-energy, funny, and gay, all of which I will come to associate with men in health care. His little Yorkie, who comes to work with him every day in a cable-knit sweater, wanders the halls depositing tootsie rolls. The Yorkie is not popular. A dog in fine-knit clothing is an irritating reminder that, as a toothless gentleman from the Deep South tells me, "animals are treated better than some people."

My boss never looks down as he walks by. If one of the sassier nurse assistants points out a dropping, he just laughs his booming laugh about "that little stinker" and keeps walking. I, on the other hand, scan continuously and drop to my pantyhosed knees at the first sight of clean-up duty, mortified to be identified as management.

In general, my boss's approach is to look up while mine is to look down. He starts with money, the receivables, bringing in his own shining star to collect on bills that have been ignored for years. He puts in a new linoleum floor and updates the décor of the building in muted pistachio and peach. When I am the administrator of my own building, I will wish I'd watched him more.

My instinct is to connect, connect, always connect, to make myself valuable by meeting people's needs. I want to take care of everyone. I want to smooth operations, resolve problems, and correct inefficiencies. "Boss" means I get things done, but "the boss," or, more precisely, "the underboss," is a role I misunderstand. In reality it is to do those things that only my position can do, namely organize, supervise, and manage the departments under my purview. Instead, or rather blurred with, I clean up spills and answer call lights—provide a drink of water, remove a food tray—because I want to be all things to all people. A nurse assistant asks me if they've changed the regulations, and do administrators have to answer call lights now. I am still so green, I take it as a compliment.

Urban cultural dynamics are a crash course in politics, race relations, economics, fashion, music, and, my especial favorite, language. The first time I hear the activities director say "props," my ears tingle.

"You mean like props on a stage?" I ask in all innocence.

"No!" He laughs, and I wonder if anyone has ever asked him that before. "Props is someone getting their proper respects... their propers...their props."

I am a sponge in this new world. I love everything about it. I have nothing in common with it background-, race-, or culture-wise, yet it feels like coming home. There is a genuine fit for me here, if not in their eyes, at least in mine. I relate, or think I do, to the toughness of the women, the confidence, the cool, the swagger.

When I hear the sentiment expressed by mothers, which I do over and over, "I brought you into this world, I'll take you out," it dovetails perfectly with my take-no-prisoners attitude.

They peel back my resistance to Jesus without even trying. Because they like him, I'm willing to give him a second look. Even the youngest staff have more maturity than I do, and more life wisdom than any college graduates I know. What emerges is their background in bible-believing churches. Peace and wisdom, fruits of the gospel I will someday embrace, abound in this world.

I don't yet think of it as anything that applies to me personally, but it's enough to put the Goddess in a different light. I sense a broader, higher truth beyond her. My tarot readings will continue for many years, but my interest in paganism will shrink to just the cards, an enduring love that will claim a permanent piece of my heart long after the cards are no longer part of my life.

Most precious, most enduring, is the impact on how I see my mother through African-American eyes. I hold the white, middle-class, college-educated view that parents are stupid. My exposure to a culture with intense respect for mothers opens my eyes, sheepishly, to the near sacredness of the mother-child relationship, whether or not she is mother of the year, which mine certainly is not. This one shift will act as compass, true north, for all my future thinking.

I want to be part of this world. I think I am. At least I think I fit better here than I did in the white world. Black men seem just fine with my strong personality and big girl curves. Black women I see at work, well, I'm the boss. I'm not seasoned enough to realize that being the boss changes how people treat me. I'm still just trying to connect. Some of them must like me, surely, or at least feel comfortable with me. A few, maybe, feel sorry for me.

A shy, light-skinned nurse in a ponytail gives me six hours of videotape on The Rapture. I actually watch two hours of it to be polite, but can't make myself watch the rest, even though the lead actress's last name is Plumb and looks like Jan from The Brady Bunch, my favorite childhood show. Work is awkward after I return the videos. I can only imagine she shared them with me because she cares about my eternal soul, but at this point, she cares more than I do, and I'm just embarrassed that she thinks I need help.

A middle-aged manager with a pixie haircut and a large backside invites me to her Pentecostal church the night she is ordained a minister. She speaks in tongues, and the service lasts a stupefying three hours. Afterward she grabs me in a big wonderful hug, and I get red lipstick on her pale green suit. I'm afraid to tell her.

The most exhilarating and confusing episode takes place at a local fashion show, on Mother's Day no less, where I am the only white woman in the entire nightclub. I will wonder for years afterward why she thinks to ask me, probably for the vanilla flavor, but one of the nurse assistants invites me to take part.

Denise is one of the toughest women I've ever seen; she introduces me to six even tougher-looking models, one of whom will be murdered in a few months. I am excited but also pretending furiously that I am totally cool, not at all intimidated.

Sweet Jimmie's, one of the oldest clubs in Oakland, is playing Brandy's "Baby" as we take our first strut down the catwalk, wearing the sexiest dresses first, mine a short, dark-green number with lacy décolletage. The second round is to be casual wear. I change quickly, but some of the larger women are struggling into their next outfit. One of them, a metro bus driver, asks me to zip her up. So excited, I move too quickly and break the zipper, somewhere between her ample backside and her fleshy neck.

"Oh, no she di'int," snaps Mary as she hears my sharp intake of breath.

The other models clamor around us.

"Oh, yes she did, Girl! What you gon do now?"

"That white girl done messed yo dress all up. I tol' you not to have no white girls!"

"Over here, honey, I got me some pins."

My red-faced apology pierces the din. "I'm so sorry, I'm really so sorry, I pulled it up too quickly."

I'm definitely not cool anymore.

They turn on me in one motion like a school of angry fish.

"Mm-hmm, you jes racial, don wan us black girls lookin' good," says the one pinning Mary's dress together.

"What?" I am genuinely shocked, stunned that they don't believe me. "It was an accident!"

"Well you betta watch yoself tonight cuz we gon see you later, mm-hmm."

Mary purses her lips with a head toss to make the point.

Denise has been an angry but silent fish until now.

"Girl, you can't cut her! She my boss!"

Her voice is full of disgust, for me I'm sure.

Mary tosses her head at Denise this time.

"Well I betta not see her up in this club no more, ya feel me?"

Mary's eyes make the point. She flings her head one last time in my direction.

I bolt, leaving my beautiful green dress behind, frightened but at the same time proud that I walked, and survived, the show. I still want to be part of this world, still think I am.

Music—rap, hip hop, and R&B specifically—is the next seduction. Oakland is exploding with new groups. En Vogue, Too $hort, Digital Underground, and MC Hammer walk the same streets I do. I follow Humpty Hump out of an ice-cream store on Piedmont Avenue, starstruck. I dawdle over lunch in a Chinese restaurant because Too $hort is at the next table. I find my sexy in this music, driven by the beat, fascinated by the lyrics. The life experience poured into each song is so different from my own, and I want to inhale it, try it on inside my head, stand in someone else's shoes.

I begin to hit the club scene every weekend, my favorite The O Club in San Francisco, the height of hip hop edge. No one has to teach me how to dance; whatever flows out of me is so natural, so joyful, that a woman in the restroom tells me, "I like your enthusiasm when you dance." It is the highest high

I will ever have, the thing I'm sure I was born to do. I have no shortage of partners.

The O Club gives me an excuse to buy a new dress every week. Its unwritten dress code has the men in fashion suits, flashy ties, and shiny shoes. After a wild night of "Return of the Mack" and "This Is How We Do It," the guy I've been dancing with says he wants to shows me the real him: T-shirt, jeans, and Birkenstocks. He begs me to come back to his house so he can change, which means back to west Oakland, even scarier than east Oakland. Still light on personal boundaries, I follow him in my car.

While I'm waiting for Birkenstock guy in the living room, his roommate comes home, a tiny, mean-looking woman with a black-as-night face. There is nothing soft about her. Her hair is pulled back in a tight bun, no makeup, and she's wearing a big man's white T-shirt tucked into her jeans. We each freeze when we see the other. She glares at me balefully, as though daring me to really be there.

I am—a dollar late and a day short—instantaneously alert to the danger of being in a strange house, in a strange neighborhood, with a guy I just met, and no one knows where I am. Either dumb luck or a guardian angel works its magic, and Birkenstock guy comes out of his room just then. His entrance breaks the roommate's grip on me, and I seize the chance.

"I am so sorry, I'm really not feeling well. I need to get going."

Eyes in the back of my head patrol the scene until I'm in my car with the door locked. Grateful to be safe I am, but the experience hardly makes a dent in the new, sexy me. Mostly what I'm thinking is how much I liked him better in the suit. I won't follow a man to west Oakland again, but in only a week, I will get in a car with a man I've known for only an hour. It will be hard to forgive myself, later, for the head-shakingly bad judgment, a decision that could but doesn't end badly, at least not from my current point of view. Also later, it will form a link in the chain of life experiences that show just how tenderly I am watched over.

Curtis is a fabulous dancer with caramel skin and sexy stubble splashed in CK One. When the club closes, we're not ready to stop dancing and get in my car—a 1987 Toyota Corolla I proudly bought new by paying sticker when I was twenty-two—to search out another club. "Brick House" is blaring from the speakers, and Curtis is telling me the best clubs for dancing. I am shifting into third when I hear Curtis say, ". . . my wife . . . " It brings me up short. I slide the smooth round knob into neutral and pull over to look at him.

"Does she know you're here with me?"

My curiosity is sincere, the question ludicrous only in retrospect.

Curtis smiles archly.

"No . . . is that a problem?"

The chain of association forms itself quickly in my mind. She doesn't know. That means he's cheating. That makes me a mistress. Mistresses want to break up marriages. I don't want to marry him. I just want to have fun for a while. No, it's not a problem.

"No," I hit the ball back, "not if it's not a problem for you."

Having stepped through the door marked "adultery," I am in massively uncharted territory, curious more than anything.

"Where does your wife think you are every weekend?"

"We do our own thing. She doesn't like to dance, and she knows I do."

Curtis strokes his beard with a half smile, and I notice his long fingernails, longer than mine, about a quarter inch on each finger. I know a long pinkie fingernail is for scooping cocaine. I know long fingernails on one hand are for plucking guitar strings. I don't know why Curtis needs ten long fingernails. Normally, it would be a deal breaker, but he is sexy enough to pull it off. He pulls off a lot of things.

"How many times have you done this before?" I quiz him.

Again the arched smile.

"A few."

The next time I see Zeke, my rock, I hand him the decision.

"Do you think it's wrong for me to date a married man?"

"No," Zeke comes back quickly, "I would tell you if I thought it was wrong. You're not trying to break up his marriage are you?"

"No, absolutely not. I just want to have some fun."

"Nope, don't see a problem."

It's not Zeke's fault that I date a married man. It's not Zeke's fault that I date him for eight months of mind-blowing adultery. It's my fault that I give Zeke the power to green light a decision I have ambivalence about. I wouldn't have asked the question if I didn't have my doubts.

Everything else I've done, and everything I've yet to do, I've done and do with a clear conscience. I will one day decide that most of it was tragically misguided, but I will brush the errors with compassion. My decision to date Curtis stands apart because I already know somewhere, by some faint light inside, that it's wrong. That light, that knowing, is swallowed up in the pleasurably abundant lust of dancing, drinking, and dalliance.

When all of my repenting is over, and I will repent for this more than anything except my abortion, I will be left with a secret lingering satisfaction. I am a sucker for uncharted territory, for fresh powder, for multilayered life experience. I will regret the adultery deeply, repent for it mightily, but will hold on to the flickers of delight, unable to completely regret the experience.

Curtis and I go dancing every weekend. He is handsome and charming and everything a cheater should be, but I still have no shortage of partners. I'm surprised to learn he thinks we are exclusive.

"That's ridiculous," I inform him, quite sure of myself on this particular point. "You're cheating on your wife, not committing to me. And I'm certainly not committing to you!"

"I know, I know," Curtis rushes, "it's on me, baby, I'll deal with it."

Curtis is forced to deal with it quickly because I meet Joseph soon after, also at The O Club. Unwritten dress code or not, Joseph isn't someone easily barred at the door. He stands out from the other men, his wardrobe limited, I will come to find out, because he has just been released from prison. Broad-shouldered and brooding, he catches my eye in his jeans and button down shirt, untucked, and an afro, noticeably out of step with the fades on just about every other man. Still light, or perhaps even lighter now, on personal boundaries, I quickly accept an invitation to his home.

I can't articulate it coherently yet, but what I am drawn to in anyone is the mix of light and dark. All good, not that it exists, is boring. All bad, not that it exists, is repulsive. The most fascinating people are either good with tragic flaws or bad with heroic impulses. I'm captivated by the paradox.

Joseph is a thug who irons his jeans; a boy-man who is shyly proud of his graduation certificate from drug diversion; a monsteresque boyfriend, I will soon learn, who always requests a certain bowl when he eats at my house, a sweet, white dish with ceramic apples around the edges that he says reminds him of his childhood.

I can't say why illegal activity makes him so attractive, attractive in a post-incarceration kind of way. His hard-edged life reeks masculinity, the elixir I didn't realize I was so hungry for, and evokes the fullness of my femininity because it permits the fullness of my strength, this fullness the secret, apparently, to being all woman.

Many years from now, when my mother and I will be friendly enough to have lunch, she will tell me, "Honey, you don't have to marry a smart man, but God help him, he better be strong."

I'm up front with Joseph that I date other men, a fact that amuses him enormously.

"You a white woman and you play black men. You a playa!"

He shakes his head, laughing.

I get Joseph a job at the nursing home in Housekeeping, a shortsighted if not outright idiotic thing to do. I'm not thinking through much of anything right now, so what I will do when we break up, which is a matter of weeks, is not on my radar. With his first paycheck, he buys me an enormous bouquet of flowers to thank me—so, so, romantic. For half a minute, my cup runneth over. Then it all screeches to a stop when Joseph and I stumble onto Curtis and his wife out to breakfast one Saturday morning.

As soon as we step inside the grimy diner, I spot Curtis at the counter with a woman I instantly know is his wife. Joseph, senses honed panther-like in prison, catches my stiffening and follows my eyes to the counter. He shakes his head in that amused way, clearly understanding. All through our grits and eggs, I am on fire with pretending things are fine, but inside, I am racked with guilt that I've intruded on Curtis's world. He calls me that night.

"Curtis! I feel awful! I would never have come to that restaurant if I'd known you'd be there with your wife!"

It could have been so hurtful to his wife, I am just sick about it.

"Who was that guy?"

Curtis sounds angry.

"What?"

I feel whiplashed. Curtis doesn't care that I saw him with his wife, he cares only that he saw me with Joseph.

"Who was he?"

Curtis is more insistent now.

"What difference does it make? I thought we were cool about all that."

I'm annoyed that this is coming up again. I am, as Joseph put it, a player right now, and I've made that clear to everyone. I am available, but only for cheap and tawdry fun.

"No matter, no matter . . . how you doin' tonight?"

Curtis suddenly switches personalities, all sweetness and honey.

I ignore the unsettled feeling in my gut, and we dance and drink, a lot, the next night. Back at my place afterward, Curtis brings it up again. He seems embarrassed as he scratches his beard with those long-nailed fingers and chuckles behind his hand.

"Yo, I told my homie we was gonna have to mess you up. Ain't that crazy, baby?"

"Mess me up? What are you talking about?"

I know what mess me up means, but it can't be happening to me.

"When I saw you with that guy the other day . . . I was gonna mess you up. But I tol' myself no, don't do it!"

He laughs, apparently pleased with himself and his decision to leave my face unscarred and my body in working order.

Fireworks go off in my head, but I hold still so he can't tell what I'm thinking. I'm in way over my head here. This guy is dangerous.

"Well, good for you," I say languidly. "You know what?" I stretch and yawn, convincingly I hope. "I'm really beat. Would you mind if we called it a night?"

"Sure, baby, no problem."

Curtis oozes self-satisfaction.

"I'll call you tomorrow," he says.

I let him kiss me on the cheek, and it's the last time I ever see him. Whatever has compelled me to this point with Curtis is quashed, and I close the door on him, adultery, and men who share with me their fantasies of hurting me. It seems that boundaries are a long time coming for me, but when I set them, they're set in stone, at least when it comes to men. I will wish, desperately, that I could be as strong with the female quicksand right around the corner.

Joseph and I begin to fade also. After I've heard all his prison stories, he doesn't have much to say, and he isn't at all interested in tarot. We really have nothing in common except the sweet, white bowl with ceramic apples. He doesn't take it well when I suggest we go our separate ways. I don't even think he likes me that much, so I figure either his ego is bruised or he needs my connections at work. This is the part I didn't think through when I got him the job, the awkward ex-boyfriend who happens to be a thug and is now buffing the floor outside my office. Fortunately for me, Joseph is a no-show the next day and is let go, a huge relief and another life lesson, the hip hop version of "don't dip your pen in the company ink."

Then "187" pops up on my pager. I know from rap songs that 187 is code for murder, specifically California Penal Code

Section 187, "the unlawful killing of a human being, or a fetus, with malice aforethought." I'm sure it's a mistake, but there it is again, and twice more before lunch. I need someone else to look at this, someone young and hip like the activities director's assistant, a cute little Tony Braxton look-alike in too much perfume, bright-red lipstick, and embarrassingly sloppy cleavage.

"He sayin' he gon kill you," she translates on the run, pushing another resident in another wheelchair to another activity in the dining room.

"Kill me?"

The words sound like a bad dream.

"Who? Who wants to kill me?"

"Whoever be mad at you right now," she calls over her shoulder.

I know Curtis isn't mad. He's a lover not a fighter and moved on to his next girlfriend already. I know only one person mad enough to send that code, and he's already served time in prison. More head-shakingly bad judgment. He knows where I work. He knows where I live. He wants to kill me.

TEN

*"I don't like people who have never fallen or stumbled.
Their virtue is lifeless and it isn't of much value.
Life hasn't revealed its beauty to them."*
—BORIS PASTERNAK

Joseph wants to kill me. I have no idea where to turn; I am unmoored, no parents to speak of, no Curtis, no school of angry fish. Zeke is still around, but murder by thug isn't his bailiwick. The number 187 on my pager isn't enough to go to the police with, and I'm not sure they can trace the page anyway.

Fear pulls at me, the kind of fear a child feels in the dark with scary monsters, the kind that makes me wish I had a mother. Then, like a night-light softens the dark, an image softens my fear, the image of a motherly lesbian named Coral. In the vein of Queen Latifah, Coral is big, beautiful, and tough—a nurse assistant turned rehab aide, only two years older than I am. I know she is motherly because she hugged me once, an unforgettable hug, a feeling so delicious I conjure it up in my mind again and again.

As assistant administrator, a position on its way out once the building is cleaned up, my office is in the basement next to the copy machine, between the parking garage and the time clock. It affords me plenty of exposure to, if not interaction with, the line staff, who limit our conversations to my friendly greeting and their perfunctory response. Coral, making copies for the Rehab Department, had barely acknowledged me at first, hardly glancing up from under the stiff braids that fell across her face. My delight in seeing her, my soft spot for lesbians—which she clearly was—had warmed her up over time. The one day I hadn't looked up from my desk caught her attention.

"S'up," she had grunted, briefly tossing the braids aside, her usual greeting, as she set a stack of papers on the copier.

I hardly knew she was there. I was reading a report from Food Services, or trying to, my mind spinning over my latest, rather mortifying duet, pre-Curtis. It had ended badly, and I was ruminating on every unflattering moment.

"Hey, you okay?" Coral had come to stand next to my chair.

I had looked up and straight into her chocolate brown eyes, free of braids and intently focused on me. Something about her felt so strong and safe.

"I made a fool of myself with a guy," I had sighed. "I'm just wishing I could take it back."

"I'm sorry, honey" she had said, surprising me with her gentleness, the unexpected kindness bringing tears to my eyes.

Coral had responded by leaning over my chair to squeeze my shoulders, pulling me to her in a hug soap-and-water clean, so warm, so reassuring that I had melted into it like a baby, and the thought had flashed through my mind: So this is what it's like to be comforted. Then she had stepped back to the copier.

Her image comes to me now, chasing away the scary monsters. I show her my pager when she punches out for lunch.

"Who sent you that?" Coral tenses, frowning.

"This guy Joseph that I just broke up with, at least I think it's him. Do you think I should worry?"

I place myself completely in her hands.

"Some men try to scare girls, makes 'em feel powerful."

Her eyes are intense, concerned. I feel enveloped, safe.

"Just the one page?" she asks sharply.

"No, I've had a few."

"Here's what you do. Lay low at my crib for a cupla days til he cools off."

Coral smiles a smile that lights her face up like a Christmas tree, and it makes me laugh.

"I appreciate that. Let me think about it."

I'm not about to do it, but I'm touched that she would extend the invitation. Between the hug and her offer of sanctuary, I'm really starting to like her. I take her into my embarrassed confidence that Joseph is the one they just fired from Housekeeping, and she has the kindness, again, not to ridicule me for dating a guy on the job, a convicted felon no less.

I try to ignore the 187s that appear over the next few weeks. Life moves on, I buy a new car, and, since we've become friendly, I sell my Corolla to Coral. On the Monday after her first weekend with the car, she barrels into my office.

"Hey, lemme holler at you," she starts off, fired up and loud.

"Well good morning to you!"

I give her a big, amused smile.

"My friend Kathy and I were parked at the movies, and this big 'fro came rollin' up on us fixin' to do some bad . . ."

My eyebrows shoot up.

". . . when he saw who it was sittin' in the car, and he says, 'This ain't your car!' and I says, 'oh yes it is my car!'"

Coral's dark eyes glint.

I'm not following.

"What made him think it wasn't your car?"

Then I get it.

"Joseph!"

"Yeah, baby!"

Coral nods big and slow.

"I didn't recognize him at first, but that's who it was, and he thought it was gonna be you in the car, and he was gonna hurt you if it a had been."

I feel sick in the pit of my stomach, a target, helpless.

"I told him this was my car now, and you was my friend now, and he better leave you alone."

"What did he say?"

My throat is tight, my breath still.

"Nuthin! Least not at first. He just stood there all mad like, then he started cussin'. So my friend Kathy got out the car, all six feet a her with her head all shaved. She got outta that car with those numchucks things, and he took off squealin' his tires."

Coral chuckles, remembering.

"He ain't comin' back."

She smiles her Christmas-tree smile, and I go limp.

"Are you sure?" I whisper.

She leans down so her eyes are level with mine. Her voice is quiet when she says, "I ain't gonna let nuthin' happen to you."

And right there, I'm hooked. Hooked by strength, protectiveness, and nurturing, hooked by the feeling I've been chasing all my life. This time when she tells me to lay low at her crib for a couple of days, I do it.

Coral is right. The 187s stop.

The next step is probably inevitable. The first time she puts her hands on my shoulders in a different way—tentative—I know what's coming. I know it's a mistake but can't resist and wouldn't even if I could. The agony will be unbearable, the disentangling from it the hardest thing I will ever, ever do, but I crave someone to mother me, once.

I don't have a relationship with God, whoever God is, but I have felt a lightness in my being at times, and I feel it whoosh away from me now, or me from it. I am bereft, heavy, uptight, deliberately making a choice I know is wrong for me but fiercely, defiantly making it. The next two years will be a revolving door of tortured ambivalence, break-ups, and make-ups. That Coral takes me back each time captures perfectly the hand-in-glove fit of our soul prints.

Soon after we begin our hellish emotional roller coaster, I am laid off at work, two years of picking up doggy toot-sie rolls behind me. The building is on track, and a second licensed administrator is a wasteful expense to a boss with his eye on the bottom line. Coral swoops in with attention, affection, concern, and homemade gumbo. I practically live at her house, unwilling to be alone at mine, and for the four months of my unemployment, I am an exchange student in a distinctive slice of African-American culture.

The Victorian house Coral rents is mere blocks from the nursing home in what had been a residential neighborhood thirty years ago. Now it is an industrial blight of tow yards and repair shops behind chain-link fences patrolled by barking pit bulls and Rottweilers. A handful of low-rent habitations, all section-eight housing, break the monotony. Hookers and johns, businessmen on their lunch hours, park up and down the street to transact. Coral's next-door neighbor shoots up under her toenails to hide her addiction from her boyfriend. It is a world of survival and gritty sociality. I am white-bread and unprepared.

The underground economy exchanges one hundred dollars in food stamps for fifty dollars cash. The buyer gets one hundred dollars of food for fifty, and the seller gets cash for drugs. Housekeeping staff at the nursing home regularly steal paper goods and cleaning supplies, then sell them for a few dollars in the 'hood. Neighbors barter housecleaning and childcare for alcohol and drugs.

Coral is the mother of the neighborhood, always there for someone down on his luck, like LD, a grizzled beanpole of a man, who asks her to help him cash his social-security checks. The story he gives her, and Coral hears it with her heart, is that he had to close his bank account. He signs the checks over to her, she gives him the cash, and he disappears, gone for six months. The checks are bogus, the bank reverses the deposits, and Coral is out many hundreds of dollars. The kicker, and it says so much about her, prefigures so poignantly her reaction to my impending violence, is that she forgives him, as giving as ever when LD reappears.

Coral has a roommate whose boyfriend shares the back bedroom with her most nights, a boyfriend who is unemployed, free in the day like I am, and gets his crystal meth in San Francisco.

My offer to drive him turns out to be naïve.

He doesn't have a car, I have nothing to do, it's a beautiful day, so why not, is my view. In his girlfriend's view, it means we're sleeping together; she flips out. In her world, white women don't do favors for black men for no reason.

To Coral's credit, she gives it no second thought. Though she inhabits the same world as her roommate, she can see beyond it, can make her own determinations.

When OJ is found not guilty, Coral is just as shocked as I am. Immediately after the verdict, people pour into the streets of her neighborhood, honking cars, letting off steam.

A boy of ten or eleven runs up to me as we thread our way down the block, shouting in my face, "OJ is free! Did'ya hear? OJ is free!"

It feels directed at my whiteness, and I glimpse, just for an instant, a tiny shadow of what it's like to be black in a white-dominated world. Without Coral, my bodyguard, my free pass, next to me, I would be an easy mark.

Racism is just a word to me. I grew up without any blacks to speak of, and where races don't mix, there is no racism. Coral grew up in the South where racial mixing was fractious long into the modern era. In 1978, she had been ordered out of a white friend's house by his grandmother, who said, as Coral recalls to me, the hurt still fresh, "Get that nigger out of my house."

"You know how I know you ain't a racist?" Coral demands. "You don't use that word when we fight."

Her observation lands like a blow on my heart that rips open an uglier side of life I didn't know was there.

"It would never occur to me to use that word," I tell her. "It's not in my vocabulary."

I ache for the little girl she was, that she was never allowed my innocence.

Coral's friends, Kathy with the braid and others, don't like me. They don't know me, they just don't like me for Coral. They think I'm a straight, or straight-leaning, white girl who's going to hurt her. They feel strongly enough about it to tell her she has to choose: me or them. Coral makes her own insanely desperate choice: she chooses me. We are ever more dependent on each other for everything, ever more isolated.

I add cocaine to my repertoire of illegal drugs, which we sprinkle onto marijuana—Coral calls it coco puffs. I also add crystal meth, the closest thing to unconditional love I've ever felt and the most obvious damage I ever do my body. It doesn't take organic chemistry to understand why the razor blade is corroded after a night of cutting lines. It's pretty apparent that the chemical action eating away its metal is also eating away the lining of my nose, which burns and bleeds copious amounts of bright-red blood. It will take a fair amount of mental contortion to rationalize what I'm doing, but I manage it, the same as any other addict. I tell myself that LSD and Ecstasy were just a phase, and this is just a phase, too. I'll be ready to give it up someday, just not today. Meanwhile, it makes it easier to avoid my tortured ambivalence about our relationship, exactly what the ideal drug should do.

My tumultuous personal life notwithstanding, my professional life advances; on the outside, I look good. I am "the boss" this time, administrator of a seventy-five-bed facility with a reputation even more dubious than the last one. Ugly tension between labor and management has run off seven administrators in three years. Still green professionally, and devoid of compass, emotionally and spiritually, I fail to consider that I may lose against this challenge.

A week into the job, I face the entire afternoon nurse assistant shift calling in sick, fifteen minutes before they are supposed to punch in. None of the on-call nurse assistants answer their phones, and the temp agencies don't have anyone willing to come to the building. I have the feeling this has happened before. Legally restricted by my nonclinical license from providing direct care to residents, I do it anyway, the alternative unthinkable. I change diapers, empty urinals and bedpans, deliver food trays, and feed total-care patients. Coral helps me as does the director of nursing, the only employee—management—that I can roust to the building.

My chess move is to pretend that nothing happened. It is debatable whether this gives the nurse assistants more or less power, but it is most definitely a power struggle I am in. My ammunition is control when it should be vision. I still want to take care of everyone, still look down more than up. Where I should be growing the business, developing relationships with referring hospitals, I make Christmas breakfast for the night shift: grits and eggs with cheese, homemade biscuits, and gravy. Of all the professional missteps I will ever make, this is the worst.

They refuse to eat it.

It is clear who has all the power, and I handed it to them on a literal silver platter.

On the outside, of course, I am cool. I can take some power back if I don't let them see how much I care. It is ridiculous and stupid that I'm hurt, but I am devastated. To hide it, I shake my head at them, all cynicism.

"Why am I not surprised?" I say as sarcastically as possible.

Backing out of the lunchroom, barely making it to my office before breaking down, I call my boss, another superstar, a regional VP in his early thirties. Somewhat incoherently, I sob the whole story out to him. In response, he shows why he's a superstar.

"Donna, no matter what you do, ten percent of people aren't going to like you anyway. Figure out who those ten percent are and ignore them. Put your time and energy into the ninety percent who matter."

I snuffle "okay" into the phone, my most professional moment ever, and head back into the fray, which, fortunately, will last only another fifteen months. Going forward, I take a slash and burn approach, again looking down, to clean up the building. I excel at firing bad apples— extremely difficult in a union building—on the strength of my documentation and the ease with which I handle intense confrontation. Where some people avoid it, I find it invigorating, a satisfying challenge, familiar even, thanks to my mother.

For decades afterward, I will have recurring nightmares of this job, rehashing mistakes and missteps, trying to get it right in my dreams. I never do, and the dreams never go away, but I wouldn't take back a minute of the adventure.

Coral infuriates me by calling to check on me. I beg her not to because I don't take personal calls at work, especially when my name is blared on the overhead every time: "Donna, pick up line one, Donna, Coral is holding on line one." It undermines my authority to have my personal life—and a titillating one at that—exposed to commentary. The more she calls, the more agitated I get, and the more convinced she is that I need breaks during my workday, which she calls to give me. I want to kill her.

Month in and month out, we cycle through our pattern; her nurturing fills me with enough strength to break up with her, my emptiness without her is so unbearable that I go back. We turn thirty-six and thirty-four five days apart in late 1996 and, together at the time, celebrate at our favorite Italian restaurant. We both look good, in our prime, blue jeans, white shirts, and black leather jackets, although my clothing is women's and hers is men's. We loll for hours at dinner, washing it down with glass after glass of mouth-puckering Cabernet. The wine loosens my tongue and my ego, and I revel out loud in the new friendships, as I see them, that I'm forming at work. Quite inebriated, we stagger out to my car and into the lowest, most disgraceful scene of my life.

"Those folks ain't your friends," Coral slurs as I start the engine and pull away from the curb.

Maybe she's trying to help me, guide me, but I hear it as an attack, a sickening suggestion that I can't trust smiling faces, that somehow I'm being played.

"Yes, they are!"

A band of sorrow works its way across my chest and into my throat.

"You're makin' a fool a yourself," she insists, and some dark thing snaps inside me.

I see Libby, hear the other kids' taunts. I can't bear it. I will lose my mind if it's happening again.

A mongoose of anger whips out, and my hands fly from the steering wheel to pummel the side of Coral's head. The car rolls forward, driverless. She throws up her hands to block me, but I am fury in black leather, twenty years of pent-up rage unleashed because she called me a fool, a helpless, humiliated fool, mocked behind my back. As the blows rain down, she wrests the keys from the ignition and jumps out. I chase her.

All I want is my keys, at least that's how I frame it in the rational part of my mind. She has my keys, and I want them back. I don't know that she has already thrown them in the bushes. I jump her from behind and, like a wild animal, bite her face, clamping my teeth so tight on her cheek that the mark will linger for days. She throws me off, and I tackle her again.

We grapple and struggle, a street fight in Oakland, one white girl, one black. This is so far outside my experience, the one and only time I ever have or ever will fight physically with anyone, and I am so far outside rational thought that it never occurs to me we are breaking the law, that someone will call the police. Only when the flashing red and blue lights screech up over the curb do I come to my senses. I come to them the very instant I see the lights, my rage completely doused in embarrassment, shame, and guilt at causing trouble for the police.

"I am so sorry!" I beseech, imploring the officers to believe me, forgive me.

Abject humiliation cascades off of me in waves. "I am so sorry."

Coral's life experience spawns a different reaction. It only makes sense if the screaming starts first, but what she screams—"I'm a good person! You can't do this to me!"—is in response to the black officer cuffing her, so I will never truly understand how it starts, why they cuff her and not me. Once it starts, however, they treat her like a criminal. The officer pushes her down onto the backseat of the squad car and slams the door. The white officer turns to me.

"How old are you?" he barks.

"Thirty-four, sir," I say meekly.

"Well, so am I, and we're too old for this."

He gives me a long hard look that I can't meet.

"I know, sir, I'm sorry, sir."

I hang my head. I think I might vomit. He writes on his notepad.

"Do you want to press charges?"

My head jerks up.

"Oh no, sir, I started it."

I flush even hotter. He looks over to his partner by the car.

"Okay, let her go."

Coral is smart enough to cut her losses. She doesn't even look in my direction, just pulls her jacket tighter and heads off down the street, fast.

"Sir?"

I wait for the officer to look up from his notepad, but he keeps writing.

"I was the one who started the fight."

What I lacked in maturity half an hour ago, I try to make up for in maturity now. I'm legally responsible for the assault. Coral has a right to press charges against me if she wants.

He still doesn't look up.

"Don't do it again," he says brusquely. "Let's call it a night."

It's so confusing why they treat Coral like the criminal when I'm the one who's guilty. If both officers were white, I would chalk it up to racism, the word that is more than a word to me now. But one of the officers is black. I wonder if it's because I was so meek and she was so out of control that they had to subdue her. That may be the reason, but it will never sit well as a fully satisfying explanation, and I will always wonder if I experienced the complexity of racism, even among blacks, or something else.

The officer returns my keys to me, having been informed by Coral where to find them, and I drive straight to her house. I pound on the door.

"Please let me in, please, Coral, please!" I beg. "Please let me in! I'm so sorry! Please?"

I feel like a child cut off, desperate to get to her mother. The part of her that forgave LD so quickly, a part of her that cannot be healthy, opens the door, just a crack. Her cheek is mottled with a jagged circle where my teeth have been, and her scowl is dark. She's on the phone.

"I'll talk to you later, Kath."

As soon as the words are out of her mouth, I push through the door and drop to my knees at her feet.

"Please don't send me away," I beg. "Please let me stay, please, please!"

I am not leaving no matter what she says. I am simply not going to leave. It feels like life or death.

"You need to get outta here!"

She pushes me back on my heels, her face flushed with anger.

"No!"

I am defiant without a plan. I am not leaving no matter what.

She glares at me.

"You know what? You're crazy!"

And she stomps off.

I follow her into the kitchen, trying to control the situation, trying to get her back. She ignores me. I stand in the doorway while she puts the teakettle on, ignoring me. I stand there while she washes dishes left from breakfast, ignoring me. She wipes down her table and counters. For twenty minutes, I stand there, and she ignores me.

The room is thick with emotion—anger, fear, self-loathing, disgust, betrayal, shame, hope—both of us magnets that pull and repel. Alert to every sensation, I feel my way through the swells.

When the ferocity of her emotion ebbs, I beg again, barely audibly, "Please, Coral, please let me stay. I need you."

It is as naked and vulnerable, and unhealthy, as I will ever be.

She fumbles with the tea things, the sweet-apple smell of the chamomile softly comforting.

"Go on," she says, her voice husky, "get yourself a mug."

She needs me, too, or needs me to need her. We don't touch, but our hearts, broken long before we met, slip back into their comforting conjunction. I can stay. That's all that matters.

We sit on her couch until the gray of morning lightens the room. We don't speak, but I don't care. I can stay. That's all that matters. When she tousles my hair, my eyes well up at her touch. When I lay my head on her broad soft chest that had comforted me in my office that day, she doesn't push me away. I breathe in her soap-and-water clean, deep pulling breaths as though I could make her a part of myself and never lose this feeling. We sit like that until I'm sure she will let me back into her house if I leave.

Raging emotional intensity fades with the night into practical matters; I need a shower. I drive home and call my mother the second I walk in the door. Never in my life have I called my mother for help, but she is the only one I want to talk to now. I tell her the whole sordid story of alcohol, fight, bite, and police. She is the only one who can really understand, the one who initiated me into this club by her genes, her example, and her parenting.

"You know where I got this behavior from, don't you?" I interrogate her.

It's a relief to say it, a relief to be at the rock-bottom, ugly truth of both of us.

My mother, without missing a beat, quips, "Oh, you're an amateur," and we both laugh, deep belly laughs, the best conversation, the best connection we've ever had.

The list of things I will have to forgive myself for someday is long, the fight with Coral the most humiliating, the lowest point I will ever reach. And yet the moment of laughter with my mother, the silver lining that embroiders its bittersweet edge around even this, makes it precious. I would do it all again for that moment of laughter.

I will one day forgive myself, but not without years of serious spiritual reflection and the gift of grace. For now, I focus on Coral. She let me stay. I owe her every ounce of loyalty and commitment I can call forth. I surrender completely to the relationship, let it be what it may. For six months, I wade into it as far as I can, nothing held back, no more ambivalence. When I reach the end of what I can give, and what I can receive, I am only waist deep. It isn't enough. I have to choose.

I can stay with Coral and have my nurturing and companionship needs met, but the satisfyingly deep physical and psychological—and spiritual, though I don't know it yet—connections aren't there. I can leave Coral but may never be nurtured again. It's a choice I don't want to make. I've waited all my life to feel tenderly cared for. The idea of voluntarily letting it go is unbearable, but I yearn, as is the human condition, for fulfillment. I start to consider, incredulously, the idea of moving back home.

My father has Alzheimer's disease, alone in San Diego, on his own since he moved out twenty years ago. Every other weekend, alternating with my sister who has also moved away, I fly down to check on him. Our visits provide no protection to him when we aren't there. He puts his plastic cereal bowl on the lit burner, he locks his keys in the car. We have to take the car away, his beloved Lincoln Town Car, the only extravagant purchase of his life, the source of all freedom and joy since retiring. It is the most heart-breaking conversation I will ever have, watching him sob with his face in his hands, "Not the car, not the car."

I try to imagine what it would feel like to be back in San Diego, the source, or rather location, of such trauma and pain. I have what I think is a great job, and it is great career-wise and salary-wise. I know I'm making a difference, and if I stay long enough, I can see myself getting control of the building. In truth I love the job, love taking care of people, meeting thorny challenges, solving complex problems. It suits me, the one place in life where I shine. I don't want to give that up voluntarily either.

When I look back, it will feel like the Lord's hand over my life, or at least his sense of humor. I am paid a visit by two corporate executives, not my new boss and not sanctioned by him, a recently hired regional VP who is not—at all—a star. My corporate emissaries come bearing news that I am about to be fired, having failed to handle what my boss expected me to handle first: the receivables. The emissaries disagree vehemently with him—they see the ground-level achievements, know how hard I've worked to turn the building around—and have come to warn me, to give me the ammunition I need to save my job. My boss has already hired a new administrator, they tell me, so there isn't much time. I promise to think about it, but I am unsure. It's not my style to fight when I'm not wanted, a hypersensitive sore spot. No matter how much strength and health and clear thinking lie ahead of me, I will never completely shake my well-honed vigilance for being no burden to anyone, ever.

That very night I have a most remarkable dream, a dream that will feel as powerful in twenty years as it does the night

I have it, a dream I know even in the instant it comes is sent from God, whom I have yet to formally meet let alone begin to understand. As I review the arc of my life from middle age, I will see that he was always there, that he believed in me long before I believed in him.

In the dream, I arrive at a house where I will be living with roommates. Since I'm the first one here, I can have my pick of bedrooms. Closing the front door behind me, I begin to explore. When I come to the very first room, a fine bedroom, neat and clean, I set my suitcase down.

"This is it," I tell myself, "the room I'll take."

Then, because I can, I explore the rest of the house.

A little farther along, I come to a room so glorious it takes my breath away. A stupendous vase of red flowers and white flowers sits next to a gleaming grand piano. Elegant floor-to-ceiling windows look out over the ocean, the Pacific Ocean, specifically Point Loma, San Diego's most unique geographical landmark. Sunshine streams into the room, filtered in fluttery shapes by long white drapes, soft and delicate, billowing in the fresh air. The feeling comes to me, overwhelming in its spiritual force, that if I had just been patient, this could have been my room.

The significance of Point Loma, beacon of my hometown, is not lost on me. The image hovers at the edges of my mind and adds to the complexity of choices I face. Do I stay with Coral? Do I fight for my job? Do I stay in the Bay Area? Through it all, the pull of Point Loma grows stronger, more compelling. When I try to imagine what it would feel like to be back in

San Diego, an unfamiliar peaceful sensation floats down on me like snowflakes. When I imagine continuing life in the Bay Area, with or without Coral, with or without my current position, I feel heavy and dark. I have no language for what I'm feeling, nothing like the answer to prayer I haven't uttered that I will come to recognize much later.

Until now, everything has been reaction. I left home to get away from pain; I pursued a degree in psychology because I blew up my chemistry lab; I divorced Zeke because he gave me an ultimatum; I obtained my license as a nursing home administrator because I lost my job; I stayed with Coral because she took me back. This image of Point Loma that won't let me go is pulling me toward something, a proaction. My first experience of knowing what to choose, how to choose, occurs as a vision opening in my mind, an infinite horizon, the feeling that everything clicks down the line in that direction.

I'm moving back to San Diego. I have to tell Coral—a thought that pushes fear out to every nerve ending, a primitive fear, life or death, like jumping out a twenty-story window and banishing from my life the one person who would catch me. I will myself to find the tiniest bit of courage.

"Coral," my voice is whisper-soft, "I can't be involved with you anymore."

"This again?"

Her tone is angry, and I can see betrayal in her eyes. I've broken up with her more times than I can count, and they all started with the same words if not the same feelings on my part.

"I know, I'm so sorry I keep doing this to you."

I brush away the thought that I'm always apologizing to someone for something. I brush away the feeling that my life is all wrong.

"I know this won't make sense, but I don't feel as close to God when I'm with you."

God is the name I've given to the lightness I feel in my body sometimes, the same lightness that came with the peace that came from the dream that I know came from him. I still do tarot readings, will always cherish the cards, but the feeling of something bigger beyond them is growing.

Coral glowers at me, tired of being jerked around. I don't blame her. It kills me to hurt her. I want so badly for her to understand.

"This just doesn't feel right for me. I'm so sorry."

I am tight, braced for more angry reaction, but she surprises me.

"You'll feel better tomorrow," she sighs, apparently deciding that this time is just like all the others.

I love her with a primitive love that makes no sense between adults. My resolve falters. I may not have the strength to go through with this. I need her to let me go.

"Look, I'm trying to explain to you that I think there's something different I'm supposed to do with my life."

I touch her arm.

"I'm serious. I think I need to move back to San Diego."

She snatches her arm away from me.

"That's crazy! What's wrong with this life?"

I don't want to tell her the dream, don't want to hurt her, don't want her to know she's the fine bedroom, neat and clean, but I want the glorious bedroom in San Diego. With no other card to play, I tell her, tell her how right it feels to pursue the sunshine and grand piano. Her reaction floors me and simultaneously gives me the rocket boost to break free.

"Maybe you're not supposed to have that room!"

I stare at her, never more aware of the gulf between us. I see in my dream a vision of wholeness; she sees nothing but a mirage, sure disappointment if I go for it.

Suddenly she flashes her Christmas-tree smile.

"What if I come with you to San Diego?"

ELEVEN

*"I must be willing to give up what I am
in order to become what I will be."*
—ALBERT EINSTEIN

I leave a lot of things behind in the Bay Area: drugs, cosmopolitan life, closed-toe shoes, and African-Americans in any great number. What—or who—I don't manage to leave behind is Coral, not yet. She insists on driving the U-Haul down with me even after I insist, a Herculean feat of will, that our relationship end. She acquiesces, reluctantly, and I buy her a one-way ticket back to Oakland but fear she has no intention of leaving once we get to San Diego, that she will take care of me there like she took care of me at work, entirely against my will.

I drive the entire eight hours with white knuckles on the steering wheel, my head a pinball machine of what-ifs. When I can't bear the strain of wondering whether Coral will ever leave, I switch to kicking myself for thinking I can move back in with my mother, which is, I hastily reassure myself, only until I can get on my feet.

Our moment of laughter behind us, my mother and I are no more connected now than we've ever been. Coral and I stop for dinner about an hour north of San Diego while my mother waits for us with a fully cooked meal. It never occurs to me that she expects us to eat with her, and neither of us ever communicates our respective plans to the other. I park the U-Haul in the same driveway I ran down twenty years earlier, open the same slatted gate, go through the same sliding glass door my father pushed me through, and greet the smell of charred chicken casserole.

"Mom, this is my friend Coral."

Coral extends her small brown hand toward my mother, and they shake, one pump.

My mother's vivacious-with-guests demeanor is absent, and with a tight and fleeting smile, her voice clipped, says, "It's nice to meet you."

We sit around my mother's kitchen table, the same one where my Xs were ignored, and my mother serves up the unappetizing food, cooking never her strong suit. For her part, Coral adopts the dour manner she uses with management, and I am catapulted into master of ceremonies, life of the party, the only one who speaks in complete sentences. Coral, eyes down, works her plate. My mother, eyes anywhere but me or Coral, makes small conversation-like sounds and nods a few words from time to time. I will myself to get through it, the mask of my face as steely as thirty-four years of practice can make it.

After dinner, we all escape, my mother to her dark-green bedroom with her yellow coffee mug, me to my pink world, and Coral to the guest bedroom. My mother is an intelligent woman and clearly has put two and two together that Coral is the bite recipient. What is less clear is what she has put together about our relationship, but her decision to put Coral in a separate bedroom is the best thing that has happened to me in the last twelve hours.

When I wake up in the morning, my first thought is whether or not Coral is going to get on that plane. To avoid my mother, we breakfast at one of the ubiquitous chain restaurants in San Diego, a disappointing reality. No more Lois the Pie Queen with grits and eggs; the local fare is mind-numbingly generic and features American coffee, disgusting. Again I'm the life of the party, the only one who speaks in complete sentences, of which I offer relatively few. Coral works her plate, but barely.

We drive to the airport in silence. I want her to get on that plane, and I know she doesn't want to. It would help if San Diego were less appealing, but the day is perfect, a balmy seventy-two degrees, the air almost heavy in its humid caress, and the harbor a sun-drenched testament to the Good Life with its neat rows of sailboats, motorboats, and yachts. I hold my breath as we glide to the curb, then practically tiptoe around to the trunk for her bag. It is almost a clean getaway.

"Donna?"

Coral waits for me to look up.

In a page from my mother's book, I carefully study everything but her face.

"Yeah?"

I finally meet her eyes in a quick glance, just long enough to see the sadness in them.

"I would'a stayed if you'd axed me."

It is probably the most pivotal turning point of my life. If I buckle, give in to her sadness and my already-searing loneliness, I will have one kind of life, a fine life, neat and clean. If I draw on every bit of will and courage I can muster, I will have a different kind of life, glorious and breathtaking.

"I know," I whisper.

I close my eyes and see Point Loma, the view from my dream, the reminder of where I'm going. I take a long, steadying breath and open my eyes. This time I hold her gaze.

"I can't . . . I just can't."

We stand there looking at each other, chocolate-brown eyes on chocolate-brown eyes, and then, the fight gone out of her, Coral hugs me good-bye. Not the kind of hug that pulls me in, not warm and enveloping—the kind that would bring me to the brink of giving in; she hugs me with the kind that protects her heart, a couple of pats on the back and done. I silently thank her for this last kindness, for not making it any harder than it already is.

She picks up her bag and turns to go.

"I'll call you when I get home," she calls back over her shoulder, and I watch her broad, sheltering back until the terminal doors close.

Relief fights with tears. I got what I wanted, I think. Coral is going back to Oakland. I am going back to my mother's house, unhappy locale of my first seventeen years. My last seventeen years have been lived in a much happier locale; only slightly happier moments, often substance-induced, have occurred. I am poised on the fulcrum of life, exactly half of it lived with no control and half of it lived with control that I have used to achieve very little in the way of personal happiness. I am determined that the next seventeen years will be my redemption.

San Diego is a bathtub compared to the rollicking ocean I've left behind, and my adjustment is brutal. Where the Bay Area is progressive, San Diego is conservative. Networking for a new job, I attend a health-facility association meeting, a meeting opened with a moment of silence that is so obviously code for prayer, I fume through the first thirty minutes.

Radio stations are painfully un-hip—country, pop, Mexican stations. I ask the guy at Radio Shack, a peroxided African-American, what he does for music, and he gives it to me straight: buy lots of CDs. No one discusses political, social, or gender upheaval, and it is a sea of French-tipped manicures. Worst of all, no edge. Laid-back, mellow surfers and their kind are the dominant culture, exactly the oil to my water growing up.

In social despair, I glean another bit of wisdom, one that will serve me well when I will leave this bathtub ten years from now for what is essentially a birdbath by comparison: The same kind of people live everywhere, just in different proportions. That and the fact that Howard Stern is broadcast in San Diego keeps me from giving up.

The first order of business is a job. People do what they know, and I know health care. I have a license as a nursing home administrator, I know I love that job, know I'm good at it, and set out to find it, something that will prove improbable if not impossible, two main obstacles in my way. First, there are exactly sixty freestanding nursing homes in San Diego County, most of which are part of large chains where someone, somewhere is paying their dues, waiting patiently for a position to open up in America's Finest City. Second, I have no connections. Who you know matters everywhere, but bathtub that San Diego is, it seems to matter here more than anything else. My resume gets me nowhere.

I can be flexible, I think, and broaden my search to health care in general. Success, or what looks like it, arrives in the form of director of operations for a hospice agency that my new boss started on her credit card. By October of 1997, her business, reimbursed generously by Medicare, is lucrative and growing. When her assistant calls to set up my orientation, she delivers a one-two punch.

The one: "Donna, I have great news! You're coming on board at just the right time, and Margie is going to pay for your training at the Hotel Del Coronado." And the two: "She just wanted me to tell you that if for any reason your employment doesn't work out, you'll have to reimburse us for the training."

My new boss is already hedging her bets. It feels like a prenup. I don't think I've ever had a worse feeling about anything, and it's only partly from hurt feelings. My gut is loud and clear, but I want the job, I need the job. I'm sure I can make her happy. We won't need a divorce.

As a matter of course, I review the personnel files and find, to my dismay, signed notes in each one agreeing to accept straight-time pay for overtime work. I don't like to make trouble, but there is no way this is legal. Girl Scout that I am—the one exception being my lack of compunction about drugs—I cannot knowingly break California labor laws. A creative solution suggests itself to me, although I will never fully decide if it was naïve and inelegant or clever but ineffective.

"Margie, can I talk to you for a minute?"

She is pleased with my performance so far, my contribution to her bottom line my first priority since I don't intend to make that mistake again. Her door is always open, she says.

"I want to bring something to your attention. I found these notes in the personnel files"—I hand her one from the top of the stack—"and I know a woman of your caliber would never allow this to go on in her agency."

Margie looks at the note, looks up at me, looks back at the note.

"You're so right!" she beams. "Thank you for letting me know. I'll take care of it right away."

And she does. A week later, she fires me for not being able to get along with black people. She does not, however, request reimbursement for my training. The funny thing—other than my self-conferred honorary membership in the African-American community—is that there are only two black employees at the agency. Again, I don't fight it. I don't want to be anywhere I'm not wanted. I do fight—and tell the unemployment office the whole story—when she rejects my unemployment claim, which they in turn honor. I don't know what the fallout is, but every time I check, Margie's still in business.

I am back to looking for work and trying to be gone from my mother's house as much as possible. I take a Spanish class. French is useless in San Diego; if I learn Spanish, I might be qualified for bilingual jobs. I join a gym and lose twenty pounds. Best of all—because I miss hip hop so much, because "when in Rome"—I try salsa dancing.

I don't like Mexican music on the radio, but salsa is different, has a different beat, a different energy and rhythm with claves and trumpets. The thrill of being led by a man, breathing in the scent of his sweat and cologne, being dipped and scooped back up, whirling through space with him in what is essentially sex with clothes on, leaves hip hop in the dust. I am soon out dancing five nights a week.

When scriptures will have become an important part of my life, I will find I love the Old Testament best with its richly layered stories of dysfunctional families, over-the-top behavior, and bitter suffering, perhaps because I feel at home there. The verse that will pierce my heart like none other, that I will resonate to and with, is Job's assertion, "Though he slay me, yet will I trust in him." I will love the happy ending, that after Job has lost everything, the Lord makes his end greater than his beginning. It is a possibility for my own life that I glimpse through salsa long before I make the scriptural parallel.

The salsa regulars are like family, and I am befriended quickly, often mistaken for Latina in the dimly lit clubs.

"Quieres bailar?" the men ask, and if they don't, I'm happy to nurse my tequila, straight shots of liquid fire, at the bar, watching the carnival of dancers and practicing my footwork in strappy black sandals.

Here I find a different kind of diversity, a sprinkling of white and black but mostly Mexican, Puerto Rican, Cuban, and South American flavor.

The best of them have been dancing since before they were born, swiveled and spun inside their dancing mothers. Waiters, housekeepers, and gardeners by day, they are royalty by night in the clubs, a different club for every night of the week. Fridays at the La Jolla Marriott is my favorite, the fanciest, classiest of the clubs where I can wear my hottest dresses, a new one every week, just like at The O Club. Even on the rare occasions that I don't imbibe tequila, I am so high from the dancing that, alone in the parking garage at 2:00 a.m., I whoop and holler out my adrenaline.

Among my new family are Cindy, a ravishing Korean, and Julio, her Puerto Rican boyfriend, a Marine at Camp Pendleton. Our trip to Mexico will stand out as one of my biggest mistakes.

Julio wants to take a group of us to La Bufadora, a one-hundred-foot-high blowhole in the Baja peninsula. Julio, in the lead, drives the guys in his little Mazda, and I drive the girls in my Camry, the same car that has already been party to my deepest regret—the fight with Coral—and is about to be central to my only international regret. It starts with Mexican auto insurance or the lack thereof.

American auto insurance is invalid in Mexico, a fact attested to by the mushrooming of Mexican insurance stands the closer we get to the border. I wonder if I should stop and buy some, but Julio is racing ahead. As we pass under "You are now leaving the United States," a voice in my head says, "Don't do this," a voice I promptly ignore. I can barely keep up with the guy car flying along the narrow highway, which parallels a shimmering blue band of Pacific Ocean along the horizon. Everyone in my car but me chatters happily, salsa music blaring from the CD player. I keep my head down, doggedly pursuing Julio for another two hours.

Much like Thanksgiving dinner is twenty minutes of eating after days of preparation, we spend ten minutes at the geyser before heading back to Puerto Nuevo for lobster and beer. Julio, still in the lead and against plan, veers off at the last minute into Ensenada.

Cell phones are not the ubiquitous possession they will one day be, and none of us has one. I have only two choices: continue to follow him or head back alone. There may be a warning voice in my head this time, but it is drowned out by frustration at Julio and worry that my passengers won't have a good time, which will be all my fault. I choose, fatefully, to enter Ensenada.

Ensenada's population of two hundred thousand all seem to be in their cars at once, all driving in chaotic honking circles around a central roundabout. It registers as total anarchy, but I fling my car into it to keep up with Julio.

"Cindy!" I groan. "Where is he going? How am I supposed to follow him?"

The girl car is silent now, no chatting, no music, all of us focused on trying to follow the leader.

"I don't know!" she groans back. "Can you get around this car? He's right in front of us!"

I see an opening, gun the engine, and shoot forward.

Tires squeal, metal crashes on metal. The force of impact is so great, it knocks us to the curb, a large gray van that comes out of literal left field and T-bones the driver's side of my car.

Despite the beach ball–sized crater in my door, I manage to open it and stagger out into the field of yelling emitted by the other driver, a young female in sweatshirt and jeans, a lot of Spanish I don't understand and a string of curse words that I understand perfectly.

The only Spanish I know for this situation comes out: "Lo siento, lo siento, lo siento," I tell the young woman.

Not until much later will it occur to me that my always apologizing to someone for something extends to bilingual application now as well.

I have no idea who is at fault; I gunned my car forward, but she hit me. Every frightening story I've ever heard about Americans in Mexico, stupid Americans without Mexican car insurance, comes to mind. I see a dirty jail cell, and dirty—literally and figuratively—policemen guarding scantily clad young females. Survival kicks in, winning handily over integrity. Whether I bear any responsibility for the damage to her van, I intend to live, to remain intact, and to keep my passengers likewise. I jump back in the car, accelerate like a jack rabbit, and flee the scene.

The girls in my car break out in high-pitched chatter.

"What are you doing?"

"Where are you going?"

"Can you leave like that?"

I ignore them all, my only mission escape. Julio, alerted by the squealing tires and loud crash when the van hit us, had pulled over and peels out to follow me as I tear back to Highway 1. I floor it, my car a grim missile.

"Tell me if you see police behind us!"

I'm shaking hard, my heart beating like mad, squeezing the breath out of my lungs, pure adrenaline.

No flashing lights ever appear, another link in the growing chain of instances where I pass miraculously out of danger. Thirty minutes later, still trembling, I pull over to get my head together before we cross the US border. The girls in my car know not to talk to me. The guys still want lobster and beer.

"Come on, chica." Julio puts his arm around me. "The Federales aren't coming. They would have been here by now. Let's not ruin the whole night."

Popularity contends with survival and integrity in a rock-paper-scissors moment: popularity wins. I don't want to be the killjoy, so I agree, twisting spinelessly the entire time we're at dinner. The lump of fear in my throat makes it hard to swallow the lobster, and my ears strain to hear every sound on the road until the check arrives. I feel like a sitting duck at the border, which takes hours to cross, the long line of cars creeping forward one at a time past disturbing sights and smells.

Falling-over cardboard shacks—family homes—blanket the hillsides around us. Squat women in rough clothing walk up and down the rows of cars, selling woven bracelets and corn tortillas. Urchins missing limbs beg coins from drivers. The air is fetid with unwashed bodies, squalid lives. I give away all the money I have left, my own problems newly framed in somber perspective.

Back in the US with a seriously damaged vehicle, my perspective resumes its self-centered immaturity. Clear of the accident, safely out of Mexico, I'm about to double down on regret. The smart thing, the right thing, conceded only in abashed retrospect, is to take my car to a body shop and pay to have it fixed. Instead, I make up a lie, vacating the holy ground of honesty I've cherished as the best part of my character. Even worse, I tell it to my father with Alzheimer's disease.

His brown-shuttered bungalow sits back on a tree-lined street. Pink and white impatiens fill the beds on either side of his open front door, and I see him at the dining room table, reading Time magazine and listening to Smooth Jazz 98.1, his favorite station.

"Hey, Dad," I call, "can you come out here for a minute? I want to show you something."

We walk out to my car, and I show him the crater in my door.

"I was at First and Laurel downtown, and this gray van barreled into me. The other driver took off, so I couldn't get any insurance information. Do you think you can help me?"

The words feel like sandpaper in my mouth, but I say them anyway.

"Yes, of course."

My father walks around the car, checking for additional damage.

"Thanks, Dad, I'll call my insurance tomorrow."

He walks away, and I leave.

I make it only as far as the end of the block before I turn around. Bad decisions litter my life, some ignorant, some willful, but this is one of the worst, and I know it now. Leaving the Bay Area—leaving Coral—was the excruciating first step in my new life. I can't throw it away by becoming someone I'm not.

When I get back to my father's house, he is still outside with the impatiens, tenderly picking the dead blooms. Alzheimer's is slowly stealing his brain, but physically, he is strong and fit, a gardener, a biker, a swimmer.

My face burns as I get out of the car.

"Dad?" I call out weakly.

He turns toward me, his eyes placid.

"Dad, I lied to you. The accident was in Mexico. I didn't buy insurance so it's not covered. I'm sorry I lied. You don't need to help me, I'll figure it out."

My father examines the door again.

"We'll have to get this fixed," he says, running his fingers along the edges of the crater.

"Dad!" It comes out strangled. "I lied to you. I came back because I don't want to do that!"

"Okay, well call your insurance tomorrow, and let me know."

He steps back with a little wave, waiting for me to drive off.

I didn't know if anyone was in there growing up, I don't know if anyone is in there now. The best part of me, the fierce honesty I hold myself accountable to, is invisible, or unimportant, to him. My compassion for him softens the blow, my sometime maturity an island in the stream of prolonged adolescence. I know he loves me, I just wish he could see me.

We spend lots of time together, riding bikes and going to movies, a hard right turn in our relationship that neither of us comments on. My fondest memory will be the time we arrive late to a showing of Titanic, and only two seats are left in the front row—two empty seats separated by a seated patron, a punkish-looking girl. When I ask her if she will move down one seat so that my father and I can sit together, she says no.

"Really? You're not going to let me sit with my dad?"

I'm completely taken aback at her meanness of spirit. It's only one seat down.

She looks at the seated patron on the other side of the empty seat, also a punkish-looking girl, and says, "My friend doesn't like to be crowded."

Again I'm taken aback but not discouraged.

"Oh, come on, don't make my dad sit by himself!"

There stands my father, gentle soul, old man, sympathetic character. Between his sweetness and my intensity, the intensity that made Zeke want someone with the volume turned down next time, the punkish girl slowly, grudgingly, rises, and the entire theater erupts in applause. Apparently, she had been asked before, and not just once. I will revisit that scene with pleasure in the years to come, especially when my father is no longer able to go to movies, or to speak.

I take him every Sunday to the Presbyterian church he has attended for forty years, ever since he converted from Christian Science. My desire is not for Presbyterianism but to protect him from the formerly realistic expectations of his fellow parishioners, he a silent giant of the congregation who was once an elder and deacon.

The fruits of Christianity that I witnessed in the young black nursing home staff make me neutral rather than hostile in my father's church, the same church in which I was baptized as an infant and confirmed at the age of twelve. A rather spartan religious experience, at least the way we practiced it, church was from nine to ten on Sunday morning with no carryover of any kind during the week. Patriarchal, white, male gods make me queasy, but I appreciate our church's confirmation process, which includes the direction to visit another faith that we might better understand our own. I had chosen a synagogue, my first taste of religion as the very fabric of life, an idea that will one day guide me home.

When I'm not with my dad or at the gym, I look for work, a most discouraging process. The jobs I'm qualified for, not that I get interviews, pay a third less than they would in San Francisco, a benefit—for employers—of the "sunshine tax," the idea that people are willing to accept lower earnings in places with an attractive climate. Over shots of tequila, I tell Cindy about it.

"I don't know what I'm going to do! I cannot find a job!"

A nice-looking Puerto Rican, an engineer at Hewlett Packard, leans over from the barstool next to me.

"Excuse me, I couldn't help but overhear. I have a good friend in San Diego who's quite well connected in the business community. I'm sure she'd be glad to talk to you. Would you like her number?"

When I trace my path forward from this point in life, everything hinges on the engineer's friend, one Ms. Violet Lash, Liverpudlian, graduate of Oxford, grant writer. I phone her the next day, late on a Friday afternoon. Her accent is delightful, like Mary Poppins, and she graciously agrees to help.

Suddenly, in what I will come to love as quintessential Violet, she bursts out, "Oh goodness me, it's Friday, and I've forgotten to make plans. Would you care to meet up for a drink, dear?"

We meet at Café Bassam, downtown. I know Violet as soon as I see the petite woman in a cream-colored pantsuit, purple scarf tied smartly about her neck. She is chic, her blonde hair up in a tousled bun, and her elegant fingers taper to bright red nails. I like her immediately. Over several glasses of Pinot Grigio, we discover a lot in common; she dates black men, loves to dance, loves hip hop, fashion, and food. When I tell her my Libby-Janet-Zeke-Coral story, she doesn't blink. We are two cosmopolitanites in the low-key surfer world of San Diego. She is exactly the right person to help me find a job, which I hope is soon because things are heating up at my mother's house.

Coral calls embarrassingly often, so I install my own phone line in the pink bedchamber. Though I am rarely home, Coral reaches me every time. It makes me wonder how often the phone rings when I'm not there. She calls for any little thing, to tell me this or that, to watch TV with me, shows we used to watch together, like New York Undercover and In Living Color. We watch them on either end of the phone line, me in my bed, Coral five hundred miles away in Oakland, not talking, just sitting on the phone together. It doesn't feel like we've broken up, and it makes me edgy; I need a clean break if I'm ever going to have that glorious, breathtaking room.

I write to Coral, telling her, begging her, that I can't have any more contact. It feels cowardly and disloyal to do it in a letter, but it's the only way. Even the sound of her voice on the phone keeps me stuck, unable to let go of her nurturing, unable to bear her sadness.

Violet goes with me to mail the letter, and my hands shake so violently I can't open the mailbox; she has to do it for me. This one act is the single hardest thing I will ever, ever do. I don't know what I will do if Coral doesn't respect my wishes, but she does. I never hear from her again. I get what I want, I know, but the space in my heart where she used to live will never fill completely.

My mother, ultimate source of sadness, seems glad to have me home, which is better than the alternative but awkward. She acts highly stressed, my fault I'm sure. I'm not friendly, still a crocodile with its eyes mere slits, slipping ever so stealthily in and out of the house. I am just biding my time until I can get a job and get out. The day I smell cigarette smoke, I realize I can't wait for the job.

My mother had smoked through both of her pregnancies and well through my young adulthood. As a child, I thought the gas station sign—"No Smoking—Stop Your Motor"— said "Stop Your Mother." Congestive heart failure had forced her to quit, and I couldn't bear to watch her resume the old habit that will kill her in about ten years.

I go to my father again, this time with the truth.

"Dad, I can't stay there. She's smoking. She'll kill herself, and it's because of me. She's stressed out because I'm there."

"I'll help you," he says simply.

I don't want to talk to my father any more than he apparently wants to talk to me, but when he is gone, I will wish I'd asked him so many things. Why did he leave me behind when I was fourteen? Does he feel bad about it? Is that why he's helping me now? I have only my speculation as to why he so generously puts me up in my own apartment.

My mother's reaction when I tell her brings out my ugly side.

"What will I tell my friends?" she cries, forlorn.

I don't recognize the sadness of it, only its unrealistic expectation, its implication that I owe her something, which makes me snap, "Tell them I have my own life, and I went to live it!"

It will always hurt to remember the hurt in her eyes.

In quick succession, the next two turning points occur. Violet approaches me to help her with a welfare-to-work grant for local, nonprofit organizations. Representatives from all the big companies in San Diego—Hewlett Packard, SAIC, Qualcomm, SDG&E—volunteer their time to review the business operations of small community agencies in preparation for requesting grant money.

"Come help us, dear," she urges me. "You can wear your work clothes and use your work skills."

I don't need much convincing. I still can't find a job, which I bemoan around the conference table of volunteers.

One of them says, "I work in Technical Publications at Qualcomm. Get me some of your writing samples. I'll take a look at them."

I study turning point one, the man who will soon be my boss, a heavily bearded senior manager in glasses with a few gray hairs among the black. Technical Publications at a high-tech company is the last place I would have thought to look, like throwing a dart as wildly as possible and this is where it lands.

My documentation from firing the unfireable and miscellaneous business correspondence make a good impression; the salary Qualcomm offers me does not. I want to cry it is so low, almost half of what I made in Oakland. They throw in, as a bonus, fifty shares of stock. I don't even know what stock is and stick them away in a drawer. Over the next five years, they will split four times, and, added to additional stock from raises and promotions, will allow me to buy a charming Craftsman in North Park. For now I am simply, pridefully, ashamed of the low salary and entry-level nature of my position, but not so ashamed that I won't sign and return the offer letter. I will be a fish out of water, the only extrovert in a department of introverts, people who sit with their backs to their doors and don't answer when I say hello.

My orientation class boasts one hundred new employees, the largest class in the company's twelve-year history, seven years after the company's IPO. The corporate culture is changing, becoming more sophisticated, less about the smell of warm, soft cookies in the break room, more about NAFTA. It will always be about playing lunch volleyball in the sandpits, setting your own hours, and wearing shorts and flip-flops to work, named one of the best places to work in America again and again.

At its peak, the company will be the largest in San Diego, employing ten thousand people in twenty-plus buildings. Mighty turning point two—and miracle—is that Gregg Prettyman and I meet, my presence in Tech Pubs entirely fortuitous and his the result of spiritual prompting.

Gregg had turned down the first job Qualcomm offered him, a job that would have brought him to a different department in a different building. Newly graduated from college, engaged to be married, reduced to selling wood out of the back of his car, Gregg nonetheless declined because of a feeling that it was not right. Six months later, a call came from Tech Pubs.

My boss asks me to help interview, a specialty of mine I like to think. My favorite question, honed through years of practice, is, "Can you give me ten adjectives to describe yourself?" I can learn a lot from how someone answers that question; the actual list of adjectives is secondary. Much more telling is whether the interviewee can come up with all ten, which says something about insight, and whether they appear to be mentally censoring the list before speaking, which says something about candor.

I scan Gregg's resume and see Eagle Scout and Brigham Young University.

"Oh my god," I snort, "the guy's a Mormon!"

TWELVE

*"We are not human beings on a spiritual journey.
We are spiritual beings on a human journey."*
—STEPHEN R. COVEY

Gregg, six-foot-four and blond, arrives for his interview in suit and tie, close-cropped hair, and clean-cut visage—no tattoos, no piercings. He is smilingly, affably, out of place in the Qualcomm casual environment, which I represent at the moment in a barely-there sundress. He has charisma, I'll give him that, but his worldview is under as much scrutiny as his education and previous job experience. I don't even know what a Mormon is, but I know it's closer to Republican than Democrat, more about barefoot and pregnant than the corner office. I interview him with an edge.

His answer to the adjectives question—he rattles off ten in the space of fifteen seconds—is insightful and candid. The first one—happy—catches my interest; I don't know if I know any really happy people. The second—weird—is unexpected. When he says it, he gives me a look that says, "I know people don't usually say real stuff like this in an interview, but I'm just going to go for it." I grudgingly grant him respect for his honesty. He seems awfully self-possessed for a twenty-six-year-old. My boss, also impressed, hires him. Gregg, like me, will be a fish out of water in Tech Pubs, someone, finally, for me to talk to.

Tech Pubs is a feast-or-famine business. When a proposal is underway, we might work late into the night many days in a row; in between proposals, downtime is plentiful, perfect for grilling Gregg about his religion.

I listen half-fascinated, half-horrified.

He doesn't drink alcohol or coffee, doesn't smoke or swear. He gives ten percent of his income to his church and won't play golf on Sundays. The most bizarre of all: he's engaged to be married but has never had sex. I feel sorry for him. It's too bad he's such a freak, because he seems like a really nice guy.

Because I have a gift for accepting even people like him, we become friends. Gregg won't be married for three months, and his fiancée is back in Utah, so he hangs out with me and Violet, even going salsa dancing with us once, not dancing, just watching. We all go to Puerto Nuevo—I never drive—for lobster, and me and Violet for beer. Gregg will tell me later that engaged Mormon men don't hang out with single females who are not their fiancées, but that he and his soon-to-be wife, Koni, never had a qualm about it, impressed that the friendship between us is unique.

It's easy for me to be his friend since I feel sorry for him. What's hard for me to understand is his friendship for me, someone who disdains his religion and has broken virtually every commandment he upholds. But he apparently has a gift for accepting people, too. I tell him my Libby-Janet-Zeke-Coral story, in part to prove he's too Mormon to handle a real woman like myself, and he receives it all, receives me, without judgment. It stops me in my tracks. He doesn't agree with my values, doesn't condone things I've done, but there's no mistaking his respect for me as a person, or his sincere affection.

I never once feel that he is trying to convert me; it will be permanent friendship death if he does. He simply responds to my questions with aspects of his faith, which engenders more questions on my part, which elicits more of his faith. We forge a deep bond, so special in fact that I will be the only other person in the delivery room when he and his wife have their first child. We talk about everything in life, and I begin to see it all through a different lens.

"I went out with a new guy Friday night," I share excitedly one Monday morning. "Armando's a great salsa dancer, and he's smart, too. He asked me what I thought the most over-rated virtue was."

"What did you say?" Gregg demands.

"Chastity!"

I had been so pleased with myself that it popped into my mind so readily at the time.

"Donna!" Gregg groans. "That's exactly what he wanted you to say!"

Gregg shines a different light on it, not negating my experience but putting it in a fuller context. It's hard not to respect Gregg. It's hard not to feel good, right somehow, around him, not that we don't debate vigorously. One discussion is so heated, I attack his beliefs so viciously, that he will joke, but not for years, that he could have filed a claim against me with Human Resources for religious harassment. I call him at home that night.

"Hey, it's Donna. I want you to know that no matter how hard I come at you when we talk, I have your back at work. I would never try to hurt you on the job."

I resolve to keep a better lid on my outrage after that, although two points of Mormon doctrine make me see fiery red: they don't ordain women, and homosexuality is a sin. I can talk in civilized tones about the Book of Mormon, Joseph Smith, and polygamy, but my blood boils when we circle back to the first two, which happens often.

"How dare they say women can't be bishops!" I bristle, irate at my gender's exclusion.

"Donna," Gregg laughs, and I'll never forget his face, "no-o-o-body wants to be a bishop."

The designation of homosexuality as sin makes me want to scratch his eyes out. I know I'm not a sinner, and neither is Libby, nor Janet, nor Coral. I argue hotly with him, trying to get him to see how wrong he is, but he never bends. It's not up to him, he says, it's Heavenly Father's way of guiding his children home.

I throw the full force of my intellect at every aspect of what Gregg calls "the gospel," trying to find its Achilles' heel. For nearly two years we wrangle over God, Christianity, patriarchy, baptism, the Bible, tithing, the preexistence, the eternities, prayer, marriage, family, and the Holy Ghost. On the outside, I'm dismissive, disgusted, and occasionally ferocious. I hate that on the inside, I'm listening.

I feel so confused. Gregg is a good person, and he's good to me. I watch how he treats his wife, mesmerized by the attention and respect he shows her. I want that. I watch how he conducts himself on the job and see a happy, confident young man. I despise his beliefs, but some intellectually disloyal part of me wants to be like him. I argue more hotly to hide the fact, but I'm losing the upper hand. There are too many times he makes sense.

I hate that Christianity says the only way to heaven is through Jesus, hate how unfair it is to the millions of people who have lived or will live their entire lives never having heard of him. Gregg has an answer—baptism for the dead.

Hell is to me primitive superstition, something only the uneducated believe in. Gregg's depiction of hell not as fire and brimstone but as a state where no self-improvement is possible changes the concept instantaneously to one coherent with how I live my life today. I can't think of anything worse—any hell worse—than always being the person who bit Coral, never able to improve my self-control.

I want to reject the sum total of his conservative religion, anathema to my worldview in every way, but piece by piece, it appeals to my logic. In fact, after two years of withstanding my polemic, it hangs together so neatly that my intellect is suspicious.

"Your church can't be true!" I lash out. "It makes too much sense!"

Religion should be deep and mysterious, I think, beyond human understanding. What Gregg is describing to me is a touchable, knowable pattern of family, a mirror image between heaven and earth. Like piecing together enough of a puzzle to bring forth its subject, seeing God as my literal father, seeing myself as his literal daughter, lights up a tableau of life I had never imagined.

It's all about family.

Everything. Why we're here, where we're going, how we get there. I remember how, as a child, I would cry at commercials "brought to you by The Church of Jesus Christ of Latter-day Saints," always a father pushing his son on a swing, or a family riding bikes, or some other image of happy family life. Something inside of me pulls toward this flow, aches to feel its fulfillment through me.

The most powerful idea Gregg teaches me, the real turning point, is "By their fruit you shall know them." The principle's foolproof nature—good seed bears good fruit, bad seed bears bad fruit—speaks to my logic, and I examine the fruit of my life, past and present.

I'm curious how it would feel to clean up my language, so I do. I had always, since Berkeley, encased myself in the toughness of profanity, swearing like a sailor, but there is a palpable strength, encased in softness, that comes with my gentler vocabulary.

I decide to act less promiscuously with men, not even close to the chastity that Gregg practices, but to think of myself as a daughter of God. It changes my bearing, my demeanor, my expectations, and I notice more strength, more softness.

I find myself talking about these new religious ideas with everyone. Armando is Catholic, the lapsed kind, and I ask him one night whether he believes in the devil, clearly the most ignorant and superstitious of religious beliefs.

"Listen," he says, "the best trick the devil ever pulled on the world is to convince people he doesn't exist. You don't guard against something that isn't there."

I think about that for a long time.

Over the two years that Gregg and I wrangle and bond, bond and wrangle, my father's Alzheimer's progresses through Meals-on-Wheels, full-time caregivers, and medication that slows his long good-bye only briefly. When he is finally declared legally mentally incompetent, my family, no longer intact but still functioning loosely as such, implodes. My mother has always been the center; now that my father is completely incapacitated, he becomes the necessary center of attention.

As power of attorney, I struggle to do what's best for my father and find my mother to be a gut-wrenching adversary. My parents own the family home together with right of survivorship, a fact made clear in the divorce decree, but when I ask an attorney to review all the documents, he finds a discrepancy that needs correction. It is something that can be initiated by either party, not something that affects my mother materially in any way but merely a crossing of Ts, a dotting of Is. As power of attorney, I can execute it myself but naively assume she will appreciate the chance to be in control. She is, instead, furious at my involvement.

"Mom! You taught me to be responsible! I'm just doing what you taught me to do!"

Our relationship, never good, becomes so strained that we will not speak for years. My father, my only shelter, however inconsistent, is gone behind a wall of dementia and legal protection. I can't accept help from him now even if he were capable of giving it. My mother misses entirely that I am only trying to do the right thing, something she herself instilled in me, and writes me out of her will.

I grow up in the blink of an eye, childishness possible only in the presence of parents.

As I drive to work in the mornings, I fantasize about throwing myself under the huge semis next to me. In this wretched frame of mind, a thought comes: pray.

I have never prayed, although I tried meditation in Berkeley. It scared me so much when my mind went blank that I never managed it again. Praying, according to Gregg, is just talking to a father in heaven, and I'm desperate enough to try it.

I kneel next to my bed with its pale quilt of yellows, pinks, and blues, handmade by my great-aunts in Texas, given to me, ironically, by my mother for my new apartment. I feel silly, self-conscious, but I close my eyes and mumble a few words, trying to picture a father actually listening to me like Gregg had said. My prayer is whispers at first, halting attempts to communicate my loneliness, my sadness, my lostness. As the feelings well up into words, I start to cry, then to sob.

My first prayer, like my first meditation, strikes beginner's gold, only this time I'm not frightened, remarkable when I think on it later. A hand, soft, warm, and definitely female, reaches out to cup my cheek, comforting me, soothing me. I cry with the hand on my cheek until I am cried out. When I open my eyes, the hand is gone. By their fruit you shall know them.

Through prayer, I'm not alone. It is a profound experience and will remain the single greatest spiritual manifestation of my life. From this point forward, I know, know without a doubt, that God is there. I know I'm loved and watched over. The rest, everything that is to come, is detail.

Spiritual experiences, no matter how profound, fade, and their fading is hastened all the more by renewed distress. My father's decline eats away at me. He is unable to speak or write and cannot, as far as we can tell, understand speech or writing. My mother insists, in one of her last interactions with me, that he has something other than Alzheimer's, a possibility that can be confirmed only by autopsy, which I refuse to authorize, so we will never know.

I force myself to visit him—excruciating in its complex of grief and love—once a week, first at home with caregivers, finally at an assisted-living center. I give myself one week off a month for good behavior. I'm racked with guilt but can't stand to see him so helpless, can't fabricate one-sided chitchat. We watch TV for an hour, and I leave.

The agony of it all seeps into my conversations with Gregg. I flail about looking for support; what he gives me instead is a pearl of great price, delivered in blunt, true Gregg fashion.

"You know what your problem is?"

We're outside for lunch in warm, early fall, Santa Ana winds ruffling the palm fronds above us. His question, when I was expecting sympathy, takes me aback, and I stare at him.

He says, "You need to know that you're a child of God, and you need to admit that you've done reprehensible things in your life, just like we all have."

I don't yet have the vocabulary for what I feel at those words, don't understand why I feel it, but an unfamiliar quietude quenches my torment. What he said is insulting, that I've done reprehensible things, yet I feel no resistance. The thought settles into perfectly calm awareness that it's true. All I want is to make space for this calm, sink into it, let it envelop me. What I've been looking for, what I've missed in women, drugs and alcohol, promiscuity, and tarot is this feeling.

I see Gregg in hazy outline watching me, waiting for my reaction. I don't want to speak, don't want to lose this feeling, but I need him to help me stay connected to it.

"So what do I do?" I ask meekly, perhaps the first humble moment of my life.

Gregg grins.

"You get to know your Heavenly Father and Jesus Christ."

I don't wince when he says "Jesus Christ" like I normally do. If Gregg says the feeling I have comes from Jesus, then even if he is white, male, and patriarchal, I want more of him. Questions tumble out of me, many of the same ones I've asked contentiously all along, but now, touched by something infinite, I let the answers in, let them change my heart.

What changes my mind is the book Gregg gives me the following day, C. S. Lewis's Mere Christianity. Lewis, a former atheist, lays out his reasons for conversion in Mere Christianity, a treasure trove of incontrovertible logic. Lewis's observation that in no culture at no time has cowardice in battle been a positive convinces me of a universal moral impulse. His comparison of joy and water moves me deeply, that nothing but water can satisfy human thirst, and nothing but God can fill the human need for joy, something humans cannot know to yearn for if it doesn't exist. His case for the fundamental truths of Christianity brings me to three commitments I am stunned to find myself willing to make: God is male; Jesus Christ is his son; he died for our sins.

I am suddenly on an exhilarating new ride, hurtling down the highway, top down, wind rushing through my hair. Tarot cards, while I will always have tender feelings for them, feel like child's play. I want Christianity. I want to take those divine relationships into my heart, bring their meaning into my life. The only question I have is which church to join. I know I'll never be a Mormon—they're just too weird—so I turn to the yellow pages.

I look up every mainstream church in San Diego, read their doctrine, and interview their clergy: Do you ordain women? Do you consider homosexuality a sin? A "no" to the first and/ or a "yes" to the second disqualifies the religion as my potential new home. After three field trips to three churches, I pick Methodist and attend every Sunday for eight months, bringing with me what Gregg has been teaching me, something that will turn out to be a square peg in a round hole.

DONNA CAROL VOSS

By now Armando is out, Brett the atheist is in. Brett is a good guy, a graphic designer at Qualcomm, and he's willing to don a tie and take me to church for one hour each week, a relatively small sacrifice to make his girlfriend happy.

I throw myself into the Methodist world, seeking to match the gospel I've learned from Gregg with my new religious life. I can't do it. The gospel Gregg is teaching me doesn't exist, not completely, not satisfyingly, in the Methodist church. The longer I search for it, the more I feel myself standing with one foot in sublime calm and one foot in the Methodist church, being stretched farther and farther apart. I respect the Methodist faith, but I can't pretend I feel the power, the click of how all life fits together, that I do when I talk to Gregg.

Timing is everything, and I look up from my ambivalence with the Methodists to attend my high school twenty-year reunion over July Fourth weekend, 2000. Brett, again willing to don a tie to make me happy, takes me in my lavender dress that stretches tightly over my curves and flashes lots of cleavage. I want them all to see what a helluva woman I turned out to be. If Libby is there, Brett will be my heterosexual screen.

Libby isn't there, and if anyone from high school remembers my trauma, they don't show it. Everyone is friendly, twenty years of maturity the great leveler. A lot of the cool kids seem to have fizzled, whatever peak they've had well behind them, while the outcasts and kids from band seem to have blossomed. I count myself in the latter group.

Less turning point and more acceleration, a five-minute conversation with the only Mormon in the room lifts me out of my religious ambivalence. We were never friends, just friendly, but honorary Mormon that I am now, I seek her out, Norrie Hitchens, my old PE teacher's daughter.

"I knew you were Mormon when we were in school, but I didn't know what that meant. I've learned a lot about it from my friend Gregg, and I really admire your faith," I hear myself say.

Norrie smiles, politely keeping her eyes above my cleavage. "What do you admire?"

"Mostly your emphasis on family. I never understood how important family is before. It makes me want to have children and teach them about God and His love for them, and that their lives have meaning and purpose."

I recognize the truth in my words as I hear them. I want children. I want a religious home.

Then Norrie tells me a story, maybe coincidence, maybe inspired of God, a story that moves me to tears, the kind of tears that are about me, even though the story is about someone else.

"We have family prayer every night," she says. "When the little neighbor girl is over playing with my kids, we invite her to join us. It's sad that she doesn't know who God is."

I cry because the little girl is me. I don't know who God is. But I want to, so badly. First thing Monday morning, I'm in Gregg's office.

"Okay, bring on the Mormons. Set up the missionaries. I'll listen to what they have to say."

Two nights later, Gregg, Koni, Brett, and I sit in a stake center—a kind of regional church building—across from two teenage boys in ill-fitting suits, white shirts, shapeless ties, and nametags that identify them as "Elder" from The Church of Jesus Christ of Latter-day Saints. They are the first of four sets of missionaries I will go through before this is over. I don't make it easy on any of them, still arguing fiercely against homosexuality as a sin.

"I just don't get why it has to be a sin!" I insist for the umpteenth time.

And for the umpteenth time, Gregg patiently answers me. "Any violation of the law of chastity is a sin. It doesn't matter whether the sex is heterosexual or homosexual."

I can't get past it. No matter how I feel myself changing, becoming more at peace, becoming happier as I embrace the gospel, I can't accept homosexuality as sin. The Rock of Gibraltar of my entire existence is standing up to every adult in my world that I had done nothing wrong with Libby. If I say it was wrong, I lose my foundation.

"You didn't know it was wrong," Gregg reassures me. "God is not going to hold you accountable for something you didn't know was wrong."

"But I lose who I am if I say it was wrong. Why can't gay people just say they don't believe it's wrong, so it's not wrong?"

"Because God says it's wrong. We're held accountable only for the knowledge we have, but God's standard doesn't change just because we aren't aware of it. He has to have the same standard of exaltation for all his children."

Through many more weeks of my arguing, and three more sets of missionaries, I still don't budge. Gregg finally asks the missionaries if we can take a break and brings me out into the hallway.

"Look," he says, "you need to stop asking yourself what you think about homosexuality, and you need to start asking yourself what Heavenly Father says about it."

I can see clear to his soul, feel the love that emanates from his presence. I know he is a true friend, that he cares enough about me to say hard things. I so desperately want to find a way to bridge these two worlds, but there is no link. I have to accept this tenet of biblical Christianity or I can't proceed. If I say homosexuality is a sin, I lose my foundation; if I don't, I lose everything else.

In the end, my respect for Gregg and my faith in his friendship tip the balance. I close my eyes and jump, leaving the sandy foundation of leaning on my own understanding for the infinitely more challenging but rock-hard foundation of God's word.

I stipulate to God's standard but will make true peace with it only after years of praying, fasting, and earnestly seeking to understand—and peace will never mean comfort. It will always hurt me to hurt people I love by labeling their behavior as sinful. I will honor their right to be and live who they are, but my honoring will be lost in their understandable pain and anger at the standard, a standard that will become more and more excruciating for both sides as time goes by. Nothing but unshakable faith in Heavenly Father will teach me to see both its mercy and its justice.

I will make my ultimate peace by building on things I know for sure, a process I will use whenever I have doubts and questions about the gospel. I will start with knowing Heavenly

Father loves all his children unconditionally, and, like an earthly father, has a vision for who and what we can become. I will see that his vision for all of us is exaltation, the eternal family unit, husband and wife bearing children in heaven as only the union of male and female can do. I will come to understand that his standard is meant to guide us toward that end, much as an earthly father guides his children toward college, a mission, or the military.

If we choose to forego college, a mission, or the military, we're still welcome for Sunday dinner, and our earthly father doesn't love us any less, although we have sacrificed blessings we might have enjoyed. If we choose to act on homosexuality—and no one can judge anyone who does, that is entirely between God and the individual—we are still welcome in heaven, our Heavenly Father doesn't love us any less, although we've sacrificed blessings of exaltation—the highest heaven—we might have enjoyed.

I will also come to a personal conviction, not explicitly stated by Mormon doctrine but not contradicted by it either, that Heavenly Father will extend the greatest mercy to those who struggle between biblical religion and living a homosexual life, even if they choose the latter. I will take comfort in the core Mormon doctrine that no blessing will be denied the faithful, that those who choose biblical religion will receive tenfold in the eternities—in a way that is pleasing to both themselves and to God—the intimacy they forego in this lifetime.

The agonizing process of seeking to understand will strengthen my faith, my love for God, and my respect for the agency of others. It will not, however, protect me from the bitter feelings of people who used to love me, or the assumptions of strangers about me simply because I believe as I do.

The peace of my understanding is years away as I stand in the hallway with Gregg. My leap toward the gospel is an act of pure faith, the pain of divided loyalty my constant companion from this point forward.

The room feels different when we go back to the missionaries, and Brett feels different to me as well, more receptive. He tells me in the car that he might be open to learning more about the Mormon Church. A rocket of hope shoots through me that I might be able to marry and have a family after all, but I don't want any grand gestures from him that he doesn't really mean.

"You know you don't have to do this for me, right?" I quiz him. "I don't care if you get baptized as long as you don't try to stop me. If I decide to get baptized, I mean. I don't know yet."

"No," Brett reassures me. "This isn't just for you."

I drift to sleep that night amid delicious fantasies of the religious home we will create, the beautiful children we will have, children we will teach about God and his love for them.

When I show up at Brett's the next morning for breakfast, he leads me over dirty socks and plates of half-eaten food to his computer.

"I need to show you something!"

He sits at the desk, and I stand behind him. I can smell the clean of his T-shirt, pine-scented laundry detergent.

"I spent most of the night looking up stuff about the Mormon Church on the Internet. It's a cult!"

"No, it's not!"

His words sting. I know it isn't a cult. I know Gregg. And Koni. They aren't cultists.

"You don't want to get baptized," Brett says, scrolling through the pages on his screen. "That Joseph Smith was a fraud. He only started the church for money. You want to hear about their temple ceremony?"

"No! That's their sacred ceremony. Don't tell me about it!"

I want to protect them, I notice, the Mormons. I make a mental note to ask myself later why.

Brett tries to tell me more about what he's found on the Internet, and I try to shut him up.

"Can we please just go to breakfast?"

We eat at another ubiquitous chain, more American coffee, talking about anything but Mormons. As soon as we finish, I rush to Violet's.

"Hello, dear," she sings cheerily, "come in."

Her red silk pajamas match her fingernails, toes. Her blonde hair is tousled and bumpy. We sit at her kitchen table spread with the Sunday paper.

"Tea, dear?"

"No, thanks. I came to talk to you about Brett."

"Well, let me get myself a cuppa, and we'll have a nice chat."

In true British fashion, Violet never drinks coffee, only tea, always with milk and sometimes, when she's feeling naughty, with sugar.

Her freshly steaming mug on the newspaper in front of her, Violet pulls her knees up to her chin.

"What does Mister Brett have to say for himself today?"

I've shared only the barest details about the missionaries, trying to avoid as much scrutiny as possible until I am sure of where this is going. I fill her in now, especially about Brett spending all night looking up anti-Mormon websites.

"I don't know what to do, Violet! Last night I thought he might actually get baptized. Now I'm afraid if I get baptized, he'll dump me."

"Well, dear, this is what I think." Violet blows on her tea and sets it back down. "Keep the guy, lose the Mormons. Those people are really out there."

"I know, I know," I sigh, "but I want to be devout! I don't want to go to church for just an hour on Sunday. I want it to be my whole life."

Violet nods, not that she understands. She's a good friend. She sips her tea and looks through the news.

"Okay," I push back my chair, "thanks, I'm going home."

"All right, dear, call me later if you want to do something."

Violet lingers over her Earl Grey while I let myself out the front door. At home, I don't go near my softly colored quilt. I don't pray. By the time I call Violet to go dancing, I've made my decision. I'm going to keep the guy. I've decided the Mormon Church isn't true. What a relief! All the pressure is off. I feel like I get to eat candy for breakfast, I feel so free.

Then I start to notice things.

The sky isn't as blue, the sun doesn't shine as brightly, the birds don't sing as sweetly. The warm, happy calm is gone. Four dark days later, I know I have to be baptized, no matter the cost. Muscles in my body that have been tense for as long as I can remember start to relax.

I call Gregg, Gregg calls the missionaries, they call me.

"Hello, this is Elder Culpepper. Congratulations on your decision to be baptized."

"Thanks, Elder. I'm happy about it."

"How about this weekend?"

I look at my calendar.

"Actually, Elder, I'd like to wait a little while. I finish my MBA in a couple of months, and I'd like to party with the rest of my class when we finish. Then I'll be baptized."

Elder Culpepper, naturally, encourages me to forego the booze fest and be baptized sooner.

"Look, Elder, I'm going to be giving up alcohol for the rest of my life. I think the least the Lord can do is wait a couple of months."

I receive my degree with Gregg, my father, and his caregiver in the audience. I want to hide when Gregg has them stand up and cheer with him as I walk across the stage. After the heat leaves my face, it turns into a sweet memory. My father stood and cheered me, even if silently. That would never have happened if not for Gregg. Violet in her oh-so-flighty-Violet way forgets about my graduation. I don't take it personally. She gives me a leather briefcase to make it up to me. That night at the party, I drink and drink and drink with no effect. It won't be the last time I encounter the Lord's sense of humor.

I don't tell many people about my upcoming baptism scheduled for October 21, 2000. When I ask my father if he knows what Mormons are, he manages to push out, with great effort, the word "Utah" so I know he knows something. I leave it at that. My mother and I still have no contact. My salsa friends aren't those kind of friends, and I'm afraid to tell any of my girlfriends but Violet. Violet is best-girlfriend supportive when I tell her my decision.

"Good for you, dear, I'm sure it will all work out."

My best friend from the MBA program comes, an Indian engineer, a Hindu, one of the greatest men I've ever known. So does Brett. Making a surprise appearance are Norrie—and her mother—giving me near heart failure. I had kept in touch with Norrie after the reunion and sent her a casual email about my baptism. I was startled to see her but shocked and intensely queasy to see Mrs. Hitchens, another instance of Heavenly Father's sense of humor or flair for drama. The instant I see her, I'm right back to that day in her office, to Libby, to the torturous pain of my father leaving, to the five years of self-imposed silence, to the momentum of hurt that flooded the rest of my life. I draw on all my strength to remind myself that I've overcome it all to reach this moment, a moment I know is exactly where I should be, doing exactly what I should be doing.

I will never see Norrie or Mrs. Hitchens again, their role in my transformation pivotal but completed. Norrie, the catalyst at my high school reunion, the straw that broke the camel's back, propelled me toward discussions with the missionaries and is here tonight to support my decision. Mrs. Hitchens, who tried her best to help me and Libby, the only adult who ever reached out to us, is also here tonight to support my decision. More importantly, without intending to I'm sure, she reminds me how it feels to be misunderstood and judged, preparing me for the overwhelming opposition I am about to face.

Gregg, dressed all in white, baptizes me, dressed all in white, in a mini swimming pool called a baptismal font. The water is warm, heavily chlorinated, and waist deep. He plunges me backward all the way in, not unlike being dipped in salsa except that here my fingers are pinching my nose closed. When I come up out of the water, I feel literally reborn, clean, and light, and happy. I look at Gregg, and he is so filled with emotion he can only nod a little.

Violet graciously hosts a little gathering at her house afterward, and I float through it with sunshine rolling through me. The best day of my life. Brett is attentive, too attentive. I want to feel the sunshine. He wants to make out. Our paths are clearly headed toward different ends. They diverge permanently a week later when he dumps me over the phone.

Brett is the first of many losses I will suffer as a result of my baptism. Janet is the next. She works at an organic food co-op in Santa Barbara, and I call to tell her I'm a Mormon.

"You're what?" she shrieks into the phone. "What is wrong with you? They hate women!"

If it were eight years later, she also would have shrieked, "They hate gays!" but that cataclysm is not yet on the horizon.

"Janet, come on, do you really think I haven't thought this through?"

We have known each other so well for so long, surely she has enough respect for me to hear me out. She doesn't. She hangs up on me, the last time we ever speak.

My next call is to Zeke, not because we're such good friends anymore but because he of all people can appreciate the 180-degree turn I've taken in my life. I want someone to see me. He does.

"Wow," he chuckles into the phone. "I didn't think you could shock me. You shocked me!"

"I know it's a conservative, patriarchal church. They don't ordain women, and I know a lot of people have a problem with that. But I'm happy. It was the right thing for me to do."

I brace for his response. He won't break me if he disapproves, but he was my husband for almost five years, and I have tremendous respect for him. He proves in the next breath that my respect is well placed.

"That's good enough for me," he says. "I'm happy for you."

Violet stands by me even though she thinks I should have kept the guy. Our roles reverse with my baptism; I had been the wild child, but now that I don't swear, don't drink alcohol or coffee, and won't have sex outside of marriage, she is the wild child by comparison. Other girlfriends aren't so understanding. One in particular is almost offended that I believe in chastity. She looks at me like I've just crawled out of a conservative, backwoods swamp.

"When you love someone, you have sex with them!" she flashes at me, the last time we ever see each other.

I feel like a wet dog in a hurricane for the next six months, the force of the gospel shaking everything in my life up, down, or out. When the tempest is over, I can count my friends on one hand.

THIRTEEN

"A life is not important except in the impact
it has on other lives."
—JACKIE ROBINSON

T here's something to be said for starting fresh, and I build my new life from the ground up. It's probably a good thing that the only Mormons I know so far are Gregg and Koni, exemplary people who will forever be the first impression to me of my new faith. Critical also will be how well the doctrine stood up to my rigorous assault, because now I encounter Mormon culture.

Coming to the church through its doctrine rather than its culture keeps my reaction to its imperfect people secondary. I'm envious of people raised in the Church who have been taught since preschool that Jesus wants them for a sunbeam; that their families can be together forever; that Christlike love confers peace.

On the other hand, these same people are susceptible to the glancing blows of offensive personalities, unrighteous leaders, and petty judgmentalism, the human side of faith, the side that can obscure the power of the doctrine. "Lifers," as I think of them, are also susceptible to coasting on the culture, never delving into the doctrine with any depth, never feasting on the gospel, like unwrapping an exquisite gift only to put it on the shelf and never use it.

I enter the Church thinking Mormon is an on/off switch, an either/or; it will take me years to realize it's really more of a dimmer, that people dial themselves up or down according to a whole host of factors.

As people in any group are wont to do, Mormons fall along a continuum. On one end, I meet the Molly Mormons and Peter Priesthoods, those extremely sheltered, seemingly untouched-by-human-stain, sometimes holier-than-thou folks to whom I don't relate at all, the ones that fuel Violet's impression of Mormons as "out there." At the other end are people I gravitate toward, people conversant with and about their flaws, who have seen a bit of life and made it better, made themselves better, by living the gospel. All along the continuum are mothers, which almost every woman is, some professionals, some full-time homemakers.

The quality of the people overall is startling. I've met a lot of great people in my life, but I've never met so many in one place at one time. I've also never met so many gay men married to women, men whom no one identifies as gay but who wear aprons, sew curtains, and swish, for lack of a better word.

I gather it's one way to handle the divide between biblical Christianity and homosexuality. I wonder if it works.

I am embraced as a convert, a definite curiosity given my background, which I convey in shades. I'm up front about the drugs, paganism, feminism, and promiscuity. I'm shadowy on anything gay—mention only the gay studies class at Berkeley and the difficult time I had accepting the Church's position on homosexuality. I'm absolutely silent on the abortion and the adultery. Since I'm starting fresh I could just be myself, but don't have the guts. I trade what I hide but hide nonetheless. I've found the gospel but haven't fully understood it yet—especially the Atonement.

I'm so grateful to have found it, want so badly the family life I see all around me, feel so frustrated that it's probably too late. At thirty-eight, I am almost a grandmother on the LDS timeline. The men I have to choose from are middle-aged, never-married men—a little scary—most of them asexually weird or weirdly asexual; divorced men with litters of part-time kids; and much older widowers.

I come home, sobbing, from my first Mormon singles event, begging the Lord, "Please! Tell me this is not my future!"

I have to be realistic, I warn myself. And flexible. I decide to accept any invitation from any Mormon man who asks me on a date, no matter how weird, loaded up with kids, or old. If I don't like him, I'm not obligated to a second date, but I'll give anyone a chance who will give me one.

As I am something of Mormon fresh meat, and not exactly hideous, I have lots of takers. Since everything is chaste to the hilt, I date several at once; one a former Marine, one a father of six, one a never-married counselor in the bishopric. Into this mix walks an extremely handsome man, fifteen years my senior. He is standing with the ushers in the doorway to my chapel one bright Sunday morning, and shakes my hand in his big warm bear paw.

Whatever communicates itself to me in that grip makes me turn to my girlfriend as we walk away and ask, almost smugly, "Who's that? He likes me."

"Oh," she says a little dreamily, "that's Cary Voss. He's wonderful."

"Well, he's way too old for me," I smirk, casting him away in my mind.

He boomerangs back. I can't get out of my head the image of his face, his vivid blue eyes, or the way he looked at me. When I run into him again—not a coincidence I will learn— he asks me to a Padres game. Following my rule, I say yes.

The game is more than a week away, so we email a few times, asking all the first-date questions electronically. The more we email, the more I realize we're a dead end for each other. I am locked and loaded on the remote goal of starting a family. Cary was married for sixteen years, has been divorced for six, has sons in their twenties, and is already a grandfather. I won't go back on my rule, but I think it's only fair to tell him I'm a waste of his time and money.

I come from a life where I never evaluated the morning after the night before. I now evaluate the probability of marriage before a first date because in the Mormon world—Mormon men marry to have sex—the accelerated courtship schedule is quicker than a game of blackjack.

I compose a "Dear John" email, hit send, and sit back.

Before my back makes contact with the chair, a tractor beam brings me to my feet, so powerful it pulls the top of my head into the stratosphere. All I can think of is Cary. I have to get to him, have to see him, talk to him. With shaking hands, I call him, and he agrees to meet me.

We sit across from each other in a forgettable sports bar with a summertime Formula One race blaring from each television. He studies me while I study him. I don't know why I'm here, don't know why it felt like life or death to see him. He is not right for me, clearly. I haven't had a family yet, and he's already on round two.

More to end my irrational behavior than anything else, I say, "You're not about to start another family, right?"

"It's not out of the question," he grins, and I feel a chair snatched out from underneath me, an obstacle that isn't there.

I don't like the feeling, and I scrabble for purchase on any potential obstruction. I find two, giving me time to catch my breath: he's had a vasectomy and a hernia, a deadly combo for reversal. Then a thought comes: adoption. It plops without a ripple into the utter calm in my mind, a calm so complete it douses, like water douses fire, the panic that he and I are merging.

A kaleidoscope of emotion swirls through me.

"I need to tell you some things about my history," I say, and full of fear, bravado, and self-assurance, I lay it all on the table.

When I finish speaking, all that's left is calm. It is what it is. Either we go forward or we don't.

In the measure of the man he is, Cary never breaks his gaze and says, gently, "I don't have a problem with that."

Nothing about my new life is expected or familiar. If anyone had told me a year ago that I would be living as a Mormon, dating a man fifteen years older, and planning a family through adoption, I would have backed away slowly and called for psychiatric reinforcements. As it is, I move ahead with a man with whom I have virtually nothing in common.

Cary is a farm boy—not literally but in that mold—from rural Utah; I've lived in Paris. Cary went to Weber State; I went to Berkeley. Cary thinks corn is a vegetable; I have been both vegan and macrobiotic. Cary was a commander in the Navy; I was antimilitary for years. Cary's idea of a nice restaurant is Black Angus; my idea of a nice restaurant is Chez Panisse. Fashion means nothing to him; fashion means almost everything to me. He's a country mouse; I'm a city mouse. It is the strangest, most satisfying relationship I've ever had.

First of all, he's the leader. Unlike my relentless pursuit of Zeke, a mistake I will never make again, I let Cary drive the ball forward. When he walks me to my front door after a date, I want him to say—I would have said—"I'll call you" or "I'll see you Friday." He says, "See ya" and walks away. A few days later, without fail, he calls for another date. We go to movies, baseball games, and picnics, but never kiss and rarely hold hands. I'm still dating other men, and I have no idea who else, if anyone, Cary is seeing.

Despite the patent mismatch, I really, really like him. The connection between us—spiritual, mental, emotional, and physical—is powerful, something I've never felt with anyone else. I'm ready to go for it. Cary is not.

"I don't think it's right for me to take you away from a man who can give you children," he explains.

"Wait a minute," I counter, "I thought we talked about this. I don't need to have biological children. Adoption works just fine for me."

I have no idea what I'm saying, have no conception of adoption's bittersweet reality for both child and parent.

A stubborn streak in Cary that I will come to know and learn to work with asserts itself. He simply won't let things progress between us. He sparks a fight, on his birthday, and I oblige him by ending the whole affair. Much later it will make sense that—stubborn as he is—Cary never prayed about us. He doesn't need to ask God what he thinks; Cary is certain he already knows.

Two weeks later, September 11, 2001, his certainty about everything is shaken to the core. Like every other American old enough to understand, his world is rocked and shattered, crystallizing all his thoughts and priorities.

I am renting a room from Violet in her two-story South Park home, a financial move to grow a down payment faster, and she raps loudly on my door a little before six in the morning.

"Donna! Are you awake? Turn on the television!"

I flip on the television in my bedroom just in time to see United Airlines Flight 175 slice the south tower in a mushroom cloud of flame. The north tower is already burning, and mayhem rules the streets. I lie in bed, a surreal cocoon of safety, watching utterly helpless humans plummet to their deaths, sickening free falls past story after story of skyscraper windows, the ghastly decision to jump judged a better option than incineration. As the towers collapse, first the south, then the north, the scudding debris cloud engulfs lower Manhattan, a horrific, choking gray mass.

Part of my reaction—horror—is shared by my British roommate and her Canadian boyfriend. The other part— grief, outrage, disorientation—is mine alone as an American. I need to be with Gregg and Koni, need to sit on their blue corduroy couch all day, watching the same footage over and over, saying the same things to each other over and over, ritualistically grinding the shock into manageable bits.

Cary is in Utah when the towers go down, visiting family. He is startled, he will tell me when he calls, to find his first thoughts turning to me. He views me, correctly, as alone in the world, no family, few friends. It surprises him to realize that he cares so much about me, wants so much to protect me. My phone rings as I sit on Gregg's couch.

"Donna," Cary says, "I finally got down on my knees and asked the Lord what he would have me do. I wonder if we could try again?"

It's so good to hear his voice.

"What does that mean, try again?" I ask.

"Would you like to go to the Temple with me? I think we'll both know what's right if we ask in the Temple."

It won't happen for almost three months thanks to Cary's predilection for "letting things percolate," but we meet at the Mormon Temple in San Diego on December 5, 2001, agreed that unless we both feel a clear "yes," we will leave as friends.

During the session, at a point I forget, a point that becomes lost in the blurring between worlds, pure intelligence flows into my mind that I know Cary from the preexistence, that I have loved him for a very long time. My feelings for him are so intense, I can't imagine squeezing them into a situation-comedy box called "dating," and yet I have to know him better.

I decide that seeing him, but not exclusively, is my answer.

The ordinance finishes, and we walk into a room of white and gold—white carpet, white frosted windows, pale gold furniture. Sun streams through the windows in glories, what I imagine heaven to be like. Normally if I am anywhere near sunshine I have to touch it, be warmed by it. Now, because the sun is shining in my body, I watch the rays from my contented seat on the gold brocade couch. Before I say a word, Cary turns to me.

"I don't think we should date exclusively," he says, "but this connection is obviously very ancient, and I think we should get to know each other better."

It is only the first of many, many moments where we each receive the same answer at the same time. That neither of us ever dates anyone else again is beside the point. Honoring what's happening between us as more than flirting or romantic fantasy changes everything, elevating us, bringing us closer to God. In less than five months, we will be married, but not without a proposal for the record books and a reconciliation, of sorts, with my mother.

I don't know much about proposals, never having had one. I don't know anything about Mormon proposals, but I learn too late that they tend to come after the couple has decided to marry and has worked out many details, the proposal at that point just a formality, a story to tell. I will have a much better, or worse, story to tell.

Cary does the Mormon thing and talks to me about what I think he should talk about only after he proposes. I don't like him assuming that I'll marry him without him having asked me. I want a real proposal, like the one I dreamed of as a little girl. I gypped myself with Zeke, chasing after him the way I did. Cary needs to make it up to me in the way a woman's man is expected to fulfill all her unmet fantasies. I want a down-on-one-knee, heart-fluttering, romantic proposal. When I don't get it, I slide first into pouting, then into mild, somewhat melodramatic depression. It will serve me right.

Rock bottom, not really that rock, not really that bottom, happens on a Wednesday, a day I am just too put out to give my appearance much attention. I wear a schlubby outfit to work and don't wash my hair, the one and only time I ever go so unkempt. Cary's parents are visiting from Utah, and Cary calls me during the day.

"Hi there, I'm taking Mom and Dad to dinner tonight. Would you like to go with us?"

"I don't know," I sigh. "I'm feeling kind of grouchy, and I'm having a bad hair day."

I sigh again.

"Where are you going?"

"Black Angus." Cary sounds excited.

My appearance and mood feel right for another ubiquitous chain.

"Okay," I toss off, "where do you want me to meet you?"

"Why don't you come over after work, and we can all go together."

When Cary opens the door to his condo, I notice immediately that something is very different about him.

"Hey, shiny shoes!"

Cary is not a shiny shoe kind of man, except for church. During the week, it's jeans, shorts or khakis, golf shirts, tennis shoes, and—painful for someone who loves fashion—Hawaiian shirts. Other than the shiny shoes tonight, he is still Cary: khakis and a hideous Hawaiian shirt, pale yellow with maroon jungle flowers.

Cary's parents are salt of the earth. I can tell they are good people, neither one Mormon, at least not the active kind. Cary's dad reminds me of my dad, very quiet, very kind. His mom is a kick, brings her own cake mixes out from Utah when she visits because California cake mixes are too expensive.

As soon as we are seated at the restaurant, Cary asks me to follow him to another table, a busy spot in front of the swinging kitchen door—open, close, open, close, open, close. He pulls my chair out and stands behind me as he produces a large bouquet of flowers with a proud flourish. It will be important for me to remember later that he did go to the effort of bringing flowers to the restaurant earlier in the day.

"Read the card," he says, still behind me.

The card, two-by-three-inch standard bouquet issue, says, "Will you marry me?"

No, no, no! I scream in my head, not like this.

I wanted down-on-one-knee; I got no eye contact. I wanted heart-fluttering romantic; I got the swinging kitchen door at a Black Angus.

But I am nothing if not pragmatic. You can't unring that bell, I tell myself.

I stand up, trying to compose my face, not wanting to show my disappointment, well aware that I pushed hard for a proposal—now—and got it.

"Yes," I murmur, hugging him with a tremulous smile, nearly knocked over by a waiter dashing by.

He leads me, a forlorn sheep, back to the table where his parents are waiting.

"Mom and Dad," he beams, "I've just asked Donna to marry me!"

His mother, God love her, bursts out, "You didn't ask her here!" and I burst into tears with my face in my hands, unable to hide such extreme disappointment from three people, one of whom at least feels disappointed for me.

The second one does, too, apparently, and the kindness with which Cary's father speaks to me makes it almost, not quite but almost, bearable.

"Then I'm glad we were here to be with you."

"Dad said what?" Cary's sister will ask incredulously when she calls to congratulate me. "That is so out of character for him."

I can't look at Cary's father, but I do stop crying. He wore his shiny shoes, I tell myself, sniffling, and he went to the trouble of bringing flowers to the restaurant earlier in the day. I pull myself together with the help of two people, three including me, who pretend that nothing is wrong.

Cary isn't pretending; he's delighted with himself, a wry first example of how our puzzle pieces fit together. Wanting to relieve my distress, he deprived us both, as I deprived us both by pushing, of the proposal that might have been.

When we know each other better, have traced our interlocking edges so many times we know them by heart, when I can joke about it and he can hear it without offense, I will tell him that he still owes me a heart-fluttering, down-on-one-knee proposal. Cary, my knight in shining armor, albeit languidly so, will agree.

Our engagement is the perfect ball to hit into my mother's court, and I call to tell her, to invite her to my home, the darling Craftsman I bought with my Qualcomm stock, my first home, the home she has never seen. She accepts, a gracious gesture on her part, and seeing her makes me sad because I've missed her, sad because she's old. The meeting is strained, more so when I tell her I'm a Mormon. Character that she is, she tells a mildly anti-Mormon joke.

"Have you heard about the elevator to heaven where Saint Peter is taking the newly departed to their designated floors?

When he passes a certain floor, he says, 'Shhhh. Those are the Mormons. They think they're the only ones here.'"

I reciprocate the gracious gesture and smile, briefly, and let it go. I wish I had let go the rest of what I'm about to say. What bothers me more than the joke is the idea that she thinks I would try to hurt her, that my attempt to protect my father legally was somehow an attack on her. I dredge it up again, hoping that time and distance will have softened her perspective. I find instead that she is still entrenched in her view that I was outrageous to do it. We go round and round until I realize it's a no-win situation.

"Look," I say, "it's March twelfth, two thousand two, do you want a daughter, or don't you?"

"I don't know," she sniffs. "I'll let you know."

She leaves, and I have no idea if I will ever see her again. Cary's parents are visiting from Utah once more, and his mother asks me how the mother-daughter reconciliation went, the only time she will ever ask me anything personal.

"Not very well," I answer quietly.

She won't ask me why my only family at the wedding are Gregg and Koni. My closest friend is the sun spilling through the Temple's leaded windows. The ceremony is short, a few promises and blessings of exaltation, then we hug each guest as they leave the sealing room, a receiving line of sorts. Gregg is the last to leave, the last to hug me, and we both begin to sob as he does, great swells of joy and, on my part, gratitude.

The officiator misunderstands and calls out, "No, no, this is a happy time, a happy time!" which makes us laugh as hard as we cry.

Cary wants a Hawaiian shirt–themed reception. I have no objection as long as I don't have to wear one, opting instead for a slinky-but-not-too-slinky number, pink to match his hideous shirt. We celebrate on Point Loma, the paradise I had seen out the windows of my dream. It is even more glorious in real life, deep-blue sky, towering white clouds over distant purple mountains, and lush, sun-warmed grass that stretches to the gently lapping water.

My mother, to her credit, brings my father, dressed in a Hawaiian shirt that she has no doubt purchased for him for the occasion. They both seem happy to be here, happy for me, my father wordlessly so.

Two weeks later, with courtship, wedding, and honeymoon behind us, I resume my inevitable place in the driver's seat. Cary, fortunately, obliges. I'm thirty-nine, he's fifty-four; if we're going to have a family, there's no time for "percolating."

"I was thinking six kids," I say over dinner in what is now our Craftsman, Cary graciously having agreed to move into the home I have owned for only seven months.

We are eating red-pear risotto, a dish Cary has never heard of but which he willingly eats as he does every other bizarre, to his mind, meal I place in front of him.

"Six!" Cary spits his water back into his glass. "I was thinking one!"

He sets his fork down and stares at me.

I hear the ice-cream truck outside pealing its Pied Piper call to children everywhere, and a sudden bright memory of orange Creamsicles rises from my childhood.

"One isn't a family," I shrug, "it's an only child. I want a big family."

"Cutie," Cary starts off patiently but warily, "you have no idea how much work kids are. I raised two and let me tell you, two was plenty."

"Okay, how about two?"

I negotiate the number up, besotted with my fantasy of scrubbed and shiny children at church, boy in white shirt and tie, girl in frilly dress with updo to rival any bride. I dream of weekly Family Night where we gather serenely, read scriptures, and teach our angelic children to love and serve Jesus. My new sister-in-law teases that Family Night is the only fight that begins and ends with prayer. I don't care. I want to be a mom. Nothing can pierce my reverie of how wonderful it will be. Nothing until our first meeting with the social worker from San Diego County adoptions.

Her first question, directed at me, is, "Have you ever been in counseling?"

I am taken so off guard that I burst into tears, absolutely the worst thing I can do if she is looking for proof of my emotional stability. It is almost inevitable that her next move is to call for full neuropsychological testing, the county's way of determining whether I'm fit to be a parent. I pass, apparently, but am not, humiliatingly, allowed to see the results.

We become certified as both foster and adoptive parents so that we can take the youngest children—a tribute to the sacrifice Cary is willing to make so that I can be as much a mother as possible—children who have been removed from their biological parents but not yet freed for adoption in case the family is able to reunify. The risk is falling in love with children we can't keep; the benefit is fewer placements for the children on their way to a permanent family.

My reverie takes another hit when I look around the room at the other foster parents: a mélange of grown-up foster children wanting to give back but poorly equipped to do so; quasi-desperate couples like ourselves; and shady-looking people who seem to be in it for the money, the more difficult or medically compromised the child, the higher the reimbursement.

Six weeks of training later, part of it on how to handle kids who start fires and defecate in dresser drawers, I'm still hanging in but barely.

"Why do they make it sound so awful?" I fret to Cary one night on the way home.

"Hey," he takes my hand, "the Lord knows what we can handle."

The Lord.

"Hey," I throw back, "why don't we start praying now for him to watch over the kids who are coming to us? They must be in a bad situation if they need foster care."

For four months, we pray every morning and night.

I drive Cary crazy: "Where are the kids? Why is it taking so long? Do you have any impressions?"

As time goes by, I begin to have an impression of my own, two children, one boy, one girl, the brother older, protective of the sister. My impression will turn out to be correct but incomplete. I have not a glimmer of their little brother who is also coming.

Finally, the social worker calls.

"Donna, I've got good news," she enthuses. "We have a sibling group of three for you and Cary. Gavin is eight, Kaylyn is five, and Justin is sixteen months. Let's set up an appointment to go over the information in person."

I call Cary at work so excited I'm hyperventilating.

"Three?" Cary yelps. "What happened to two?"

"Yes, three, it's not that much more than two, is it? You said the Lord knew what we could handle."

Cary is silent as I babble on.

"The social worker told me they all thought 'Cary and Donna' when they read the case file. Don't you think that means something? I was right about the older brother, younger sister. Didn't feel anything about the baby. What do you think that means? . . . Cary? . . . Cary?"

"Three?" Cary says again.

"Yes . . . three . . . is that okay?"

I hold my breath.

The best man I've ever known, the only man I could ever see myself with in the eternities, lets out a long sigh.

"If the Lord wants us to have three, I guess we'll have three."

At "the telling" the next day, our social worker hands us each a set of papers describing the kids. My excitement plummets as she reads the information aloud to us.

". . . alcohol . . . crystal meth . . . domestic violence . . . criminal histories . . . mental illness . . . possible drug exposure in utero . . . severe neglect . . . speech delays . . . delays in fine-motor coordination . . . several Child Protective Services reports on the family . . . in foster care for last eight months . . . separate foster homes . . ."

My mother fantasy clutches at the straw called "neglect," a word that ironically, so ironically, sounds hopeful, benign even, like one might neglect the dusting and then catch up. Reactive Attachment Disorder education, counseling—years of it—horse therapy, and medication will cast a different light on that word, a word that is in fact the darkest on the list.

Neglect will come to mean Justin crying alone in his crib, wet, hungry, scared with no one to comfort him. It will explain why Gavin at age five sat down and waited to die from the raging fire in the house next door because he was too frightened to wake his passed-out parents. It will be the shadow behind their attachment disorder, behind the note in Kaylyn's chart, documented by a neuropsychologist, that she hadn't had a need met "since she came out of the birth canal."

My ignorance of the word will be replaced with sober knowledge that eye contact between mother and infant—which none of my children received—is the foundation of cause-and-effect thinking; that brain development results from maternal nurturing, and without it, there are literal holes where there should be connective tissue.

"How did they come into foster care?" Cary asks.

The social worker reads a long passage from the paperwork. "The father left Justin with a stranger at the park 'because the angels told him that the other children (Gavin and Kaylyn) were in danger.' It was reported that the father was frantically searching the public park, believing that Gavin and Kaylyn were missing. A large search effort ensued with over one hundred people looking for Gavin and Kaylyn. Apparently, the father conjured up the story that the children were missing, which could have been due to his substance abuse and/or mental health issues. Gavin and Kaylyn were actually home with the mother during the search. When the police department went out to investigate, they found the children were neglected and both parents were using drugs and alcohol. It was also discovered that the parents regularly engaged in verbal and physical fights in the presence of the children."

She looks up. "It says that when the police found Justin, he was soaked in urine from head to toe, and the milk in his sippy cup was curdled."

The statement, as horrible as it sounds, means nothing to me compared to what it will mean once I've changed diapers and filled sippy cups. I will think back on it often, enraged to the point of shaking when I consider how long it takes milk to curdle, how long it was that Justin went without attention.

The social worker moves on. "The kids are so cute. They're doing really well in their foster homes. The next step would be for you to meet them."

She raises her eyebrows at us, "Yes? Would you like to meet them?"

"Okay," Cary says, looking at me.

I just nod.

We leave the social worker's office and drive directly to the Temple. I have a bad feeling about the girl, maybe because I am a girl and dread what I imagine she has already been through, maybe because I sense, correctly, the nightmare ahead.

In the white and gold heaven room, I pour my trepidation out to Heavenly Father. I don't want to take the girl, know already I can't handle her, that she will be my undoing. Heavenly Father must agree, must know that her purpose is to undo me, a divine and necessary purpose, because he opens a vision in my mind. I see a lavender so beautiful I can't describe it, beyond anything I've seen on earth, and with it comes the certain knowledge that this loveliness is the essence of Kaylyn's soul.

My trepidation doesn't disappear, but my reluctance does.

"I can do it," I whisper to Cary sitting next to me on the couch.

"Then let's do," he whispers back. "I think these are our kids."

"Is that what the Lord told you? All three?" I ask under my breath.

"All three."

We meet Gavin first, in a foster home by himself. He's so good looking my jaw drops, a Calvin Klein model at eight, buzzed brown hair framing his tan face, hazel eyes watching us guardedly. I feel his gentle spirit. His hurting spirit I witness when the foster mother shows him his homework. Gavin drops to the floor and wraps himself around the base of the table, refusing to move or talk until we leave.

I am terrified to meet Justin the next day. I know nothing about babies. Red-cheeked and lethargic, he sits on the floor in little boy Keds, pointing silently out the window. His foster mother shows us his medications: Benadryl, Motrin, and three asthma breathing treatments a day, enough medical complexity—without any documentation of the need for such in his chart—to garner a hefty reimbursement from the county. Once in our home, Justin will never receive those medications again, and our physician will rule out any hint of asthma. Lethargy gone, his personality will come alive, the vital saving grace in our patchwork family, the only thing that makes any of us smile or laugh for years.

Cary and I get down on the floor with Justin, an elephant puppet on Cary's hand, a lion puppet on mine, and sing, "The wheels on the bus go round and round, round and round, round and round, the wheels on the bus go round and round, all through the town." Justin breaks into a smile that lights up his green eyes and melts my heart.

We are singing the umpteenth verse when Kaylyn flies through the door from school, adorable in blonde ponytails and a black-and-white jumper. She plops immediately down on the floor next to us and starts singing. Only later will I realize that she showed no stranger danger, and a slow twisting in my gut will bring my trepidation into focus.

We bring all three kids together for the next visit, a trip for chocolate pancakes with Mr. and Mrs. Disneyland. I know nothing about kids of any age. "Yes" is the only word I know, a far cry from the "Captain von Trapp without the whistle" my mother will dub me soon after. In less than two weeks, I go from a forty-one-year-old career woman to a stay-at-home mother afraid to come out of her bedroom in the mornings.

Every Sunday at church for the next three weeks, someone asks, "How's it going with the kids?" and I burst into tears.

On the fourth week, when I am able to remain composed, I think to myself, "It must be going better." It is, rather, about to get much worse for a very long time.

I wanted to be a mother, and I got what I wished for. Now I learn the universal lesson of mothers everywhere: children show you the ugliness in yourself you didn't know you had. It will be almost a decade before I realize that it's their job, divinely speaking, to show me to myself and inspire me to fix what's broken. Because, as it turns out, I am very, very broken.

FOURTEEN

*"You did what you knew.
When you knew better, you did better."*
—MAYA ANGELOU

The insight required for me to realize I am broken is not possible in survival mode, the hanging-on-by-the-skin-of-our-teeth life we live—all of us—for many years. Whatever dreams I had of marriage to Cary, and he of marriage to me, drown in the roiling sea of frustrated hopes and unmet expectations.

Adoption is the vision when we marry, but something happens in our numinous merging, some unrequitable hope of making a baby, not for Cary so much as for me. It is one thing to contemplate adoption as a hypothetical, quite another to relinquish forever the possibility of creating life with my husband when it is time to draw the curtain.

Trying to reverse Cary's vasectomy from twenty-five years ago, complicated by the hernia, is probably pointless, but

I flirt with artificial insemination. I long to make a baby with Cary, to see his hands and my eyes, my smile and his dimpled chin in a beloved child of God. Cary is willing to give me whatever I think I need, but I can't, in the end, justify making a baby at fifty-four and thirty-nine, can't make myself see it as fair to the baby. For a long while, I hope it happens miraculously despite the vasectomy, an irrational hope of the fairy-tale ending that will give me what I want without guilt.

At forty-two, I will go through menopause and realize how unlikely it was that I could ever have become pregnant by Cary under any circumstances. He will tell me only then of the spiritual impression he received after we broke up that I would not be able to bear children. It had helped him to move forward with our relationship, released from the burden of guilt that he was taking something precious away from me.

I know that adopting older, hard-to-place children is the win-win: a family for us, a stable home for children overlooked by twenty-somethings seeking infants. Knowing we're doing the right thing doesn't lessen my anguish that I am missing out on the most incredible, most meaningful experience a human being can have. For someone who values experience above all else, it is torment.

Into this dying-breath gasp of unfulfilled yearning come three precious children at the mercy of birth parents, social workers, judges, foster parents, and us. Frightened and helpless, they are thrust into our home and expected to cope, which they do as all children who survive trauma do, but with a searing pain that shows itself in myriad ways: lying, bullying, destructiveness, screaming, self-inflicted injuries, violent temper tantrums, stealing, and fire setting.

"The first month was awful, but it will be okay now, right?" I ask Cary.

He shrugs with still a hint of hopefulness. Five more meat-grinding months elapse.

"The first six months were awful, but it will be okay now, right?" I ask, and he shrugs again, this time with a heaviness that permeates his spirit.

Too late, Cary realizes that raising two sons in no way prepared him for raising attachment-disordered kids, and—fifty-six now—it would be exhausting even if they were easy. In the first six years we have the kids, Cary will have five operations, including total knee replacement and ankle fusion. He will lose the ability to walk without pain and will be limited to short distances, a change in his quality of life that will change his personality for a long while. I will watch him fight through grief at losing his physical abilities, guilt at depriving the kids of an active father, and even bitterness for a time toward the Lord for leading him into this vale of tears.

Cary is already a grandfather of two, a boy and a girl the same ages as Kaylyn and Justin, and finds it nearly impossible to recapture the vigor of fatherhood. He has sacrificed what he now realizes is the rest of his life to give me the gift of motherhood. With these children and the depth of their needs, there is no hope of him outlasting active parenting, the hope of golden years seemingly dead forever.

Six months turn into a year, which turns into two and then five, and finally I accept that there is no putting awful behind us. For two interminable years, the birth parents ignore chance after chance at court-ordered classes on substance abuse and anger management, requirements of the reunification plan. They also skip scheduled visits with the kids, utterly wrenching occasions for children awash in feelings they don't understand and can't express. The birth mother is essentially MIA, and the birth father struggles with time concepts and self-management, often forgetting the appointment or showing up when the kids aren't there.

Most of my empathy is for Gavin, Kaylyn, and Justin, who have to endure such turmoil through no fault of their own, but the rest of my empathy, a sour slice of it, is reserved for myself and Cary. If the kids' acting out is fireworks, our life is a sustained grand finale.

We need date nights, the magic between us fading fast, but no one can babysit unless they've been fingerprinted and certified in first aid and CPR. The waiting list for county-approved babysitters is long, and when we get our turn, they don't want to come back because Gavin and Kaylyn fight so viciously. My mother, God bless her, becomes a certified babysitter but complains that Justin won't mind her, so I don't ask her for help unless there's an emergency.

Extended foster care is meant to protect Gavin, the termination of parental bond, such as it is, seen as particularly traumatic for an eight-year-old. The delay paralyzes him, a loyal little boy who naturally wants the only parents he has ever known. He won't let go while there's still a chance and grows more angry, more sullen the longer he's with us. He feels entitled to boss and bully Kaylyn, protective and resentful at the same time. When he should have been playing with Legos, he was keeping them both alive with Hot Pockets and Eggos donated by sympathetic neighbors while their parents were passed out from drugs.

Kaylyn looks to Gavin as the parent, her learned helplessness inflaming his resentment further. At six, she is unable to brush her teeth, and has apparently never made a decision for herself. She has virtually no social skills, unable to express her feelings except through screaming, which she does every day for the first year, especially when she hears the word "no." To give the rest of the family a break, I take to driving her around while she screams and kicks my seat from the back.

Swinging wildly between eager to please, manipulative, and enraged, she is a bottomless pit of need, reaching her arms up for "huggy, huggy" so many times in a day that her voice starts to sound like nails on a chalkboard to me.

Cary ingeniously devises a strategy where he initiates asking her for hugs, and she relaxes a little as she realizes the hugs are there for her. Part of me wishes I could do the same, could nurture her the way he does. I know it's the right thing to do, know I have to do it, but can't make myself, the first hint I'm not who I thought I was.

I hear myself say impatient, unkind things to Kaylyn, things that sound like my mother, a woman I swore I would never be. I'm harsh and critical, cold and controlling, and I resent

Kaylyn for it, a completely irrational position, a grit-my-teeth standoff with her. In my mind, I flail wildly for what she's doing wrong, what I need to fix in her, the new bane of my existence. My theories cycle like a Ferris wheel.

First, I tell myself, she's not my kind of female; I'm drawn to tigers, she's a butterfly. Next, her giddiness reminds me of my mother, both of them the opposite of deep, their light-heartedness something that makes me feel heavy and dark by comparison. By far the easiest target, a quality I abhor in anyone, Kaylyn's neediness smothers me, a hunger I am loathe to meet.

Gavin is not easy, but I do better with him because he leans away from me, giving me the space to nurture him without feeling forced to do it, not that I feel safe enough with him to really give. He talks about his birth parents frequently, and I feel an awkward inferiority to them, steeling myself against the hurt that I'm not who Gavin really wants. Years after we've adopted him, years after he's seen his birth mother for the last time, Mother's Day is hard for both of us.

"Mom," he asks, "do you have a card I can send my birth mom?"

"You want to send her a Mother's Day card?"

In my head and at the top of my heart, I understand completely, and draw from the flow of understanding to hand him a card, and a stamp. In the deep of my heart I break, and cry in the garage, wanting him to think of me as his mother, wanting him to give me a card.

Justin, the only one who sees me as his "real" mother, the only one from whom I feel no rejection, is a hypochondriac by the time he can talk. His overwhelming fear of virtually everything, his paralyzing anxiety, only simmers until he his older, a tender mercy that I am spared the most intense problems of all three children at once.

With Justin, I am my best self. With him I can be patient, nurturing, silly even, something I didn't know I was capable of and don't feel comfortable sharing with anyone else, not even Cary. I feel like a mother, a good mother, with Justin. It reinforces my belief that Kaylyn is the problem, not me.

Motherhood in general is a miserable experience, nothing like I fantasized, and I wouldn't wish it on my worst enemy. If one more person tells me, "Love them, just love them," I'm going to scream. Down the road, we will stumble on—or be led to—an attachment therapist who will explain that love is not enough—and why—but for a good eight years, we slog through counselors who try to help us bond but don't succeed beyond the surface.

It never feels comfortable, none of us ever relaxes, we have zero fun. If not for Justin, the only positive thing Gavin and Kaylyn bring with them from their old life, the only one who can make any of us laugh, we would have no sunshine in our home at all.

"Why didn't the county tell us how awful it would be?" I fume to Cary.

Comforting rays of sunshine do light up our larger world. Cary's sons, one in his late twenties and one—the one with children—in his early thirties, are nothing but warm and welcoming to the kids. Cary's family time, which until now has been entirely focused on his first two sons and his grandchildren, becomes split, diluted, distracted by the chaos in his new home, a development his sons handle with graciousness toward me and the kids. If they have feelings about their father beginning all over again with a brand-new and much-younger family, they don't show it.

His youngest son opens savings accounts for Gavin, Kaylyn, and Justin, a generous gesture that gives us a much-needed sense of support. Cary's grandchildren see them as cousins, delighted to have more friends their own age in the family. Cary's brother and sister-in-law agree to act as guardians in the event of our deaths, another much-appreciated support as well as a requirement for legal adoption. There is no better family anywhere, either for myself or the kids.

Ultimately, the courts terminate the birth parents' rights, the birth mother never having complied with the reunification plan and the birth father mentally incapable of doing so. It is a sickening ripping apart of one family to make another. Adoption, especially older-child adoption, is more than a concept to me now. My children's heartbreak at losing their birth parents will never heal completely, will be at best a forever-tender bruise in their innermost parts. I am helpless to protect them from the wounding; I am their mother only because of it.

Their hurt expresses itself, understandably and heavily stressed by the county's training, toward me most of all. Children who have been betrayed by a mother take rage, fear, and grief out on the mother substitute. Their survival instinct is as strong as mine, and they intend never to be hurt again.

I read a passage in a book on Reactive Attachment Disorder that rings with bitter truth. A hypothetical happy infant sees her mother across a lake of frozen ice. Delightedly, she begins to crawl as fast as she can to the most important person in her world. Suddenly the ice breaks, and she plunges through, nearly drowning in the dark, cold water. Scrambling back to solid ice, she is forever burned with a life-or-death lesson: loving and being loved is dangerous. Our children's mission, the attachment therapist will teach us one day, is to hate us and to make us hate them. They excel at it. I also make it easy.

They need structure; I give them too much structure. They need discipline; I give them too much discipline. Way too far into the process, I will learn that I work from the outside in because I haven't yet done my own work from the inside out. The years I spend praying, fasting, and analyzing why I'm so harsh—so mean sometimes—to Kaylyn bear no fruit. Focused on her as they are, the questions bounce off the locked-away part of myself that hates her weakness for reasons that have nothing to do with her.

The bitterest moments are when Cary wonders why he volunteered for hell on earth, and I feel guilty that his sacrifice for me is almost more than he can bear. I wince that he sees my ugliness toward Kaylyn, and I witness his own version of ugly when he reaches the end of his rope. The marriage, while never in serious jeopardy of failing, loses its warmth, its enthusiasm.

There are bitterly regretted days of harsh words and self-protection, where we each make it harder for the other to survive.

Life closes down to nothing but managing the kids' behavior. I catch every cold that Gavin and Kaylyn bring home from every other child at school. I consider apostasy, suicide, and giving the kids back but refuse, absolutely refuse, to give up.

When someone new hears our story, the "How wonderful! What you're doing for those kids is so noble!" twists like a knife in my cold, non-nurturing belly.

"There's nothing noble about it," I retort, "I had no idea what I was getting myself into."

Years later, bruised and bleeding but still hanging in, I will grudgingly accept some credit for not giving up, hoping that what I can give makes up for what I can't. What emerges as my strength, and a mighty one, is how I handle the aftermath of atrocious behavior. Where I am seriously deficient in positive inputs during casual times, I am a gold medalist in positive inputs during times when shame, the greatest curse for children like mine, howls in their faces. It comes naturally to me, reaching in when they are broken by their own choices; I'm at home with dark and unbearable.

What my mother could never do for me, keeping me company in my hurt so that it doesn't turn to shame, I do for my children. I see them, good, bad, and ugly. I meet them in the dark place, unafraid to feel what they are feeling, and show them the light in themselves. This is when my voice is the gentlest, my physical affection the most nurturing, the lifeline I throw them for a better future the strongest.

I cling to unshakable faith in Heavenly Father. I know that Cary and I were brought together by his hand, know that he has a reason for putting us together as a family. I easily recognize the value of my previous life experience in preparing me to help my children. I do not yet glean the deeper truth that my children have been sent, have been prepared spiritually, to help me.

Through sheer determination, I learn the practical parts of parenting, slowly realizing that raising kids is more like herding cats than writing software code. I accept that I have to tell them more than once—over and over, in fact—to pick up their stinky socks, turn off the lights, shut the door. I learn a fair amount of patience, not enough but more, learn to keep my voice down most of the time. Only when I turn into "Volcano Mom," as we will jokingly name her after she has been retired, do I really scare them.

Practice gives me the strength to back-burner the most acute distress, but their behaviors aren't any less awful—and middle school for Gavin with its six teachers and six subjects ratchets up the stress to new heights. I wish I could drink.

Cary, despite his personal meltdown, does what he can to ease my stress, often taking the kids for hours on Saturday so that I have time to myself, something I need to hold onto my sanity, something he rarely enjoys. We adapt.

I begin to see my children for who they are apart from the trauma that has fueled their early life. Gavin has a remarkable talent for working with his hands, building complicated Lego structures way beyond, the counselor marvels, what any other kids can do. He has a heart of solid gold that he isn't quite ready to give to himself. Too scared to order his own ice-cream cone, he nonetheless canvasses door-to-door to help our neighbor find her little lost dog.

The day we are sealed as an eternal family in the San Diego Temple, Gavin shyly tells me, "This is the best day of my life."

Kaylyn is made of sweetness, a burr under my saddle since I am not, but she touches even me when she roots for other girls at her softball games. Actually, I shake my head because she's rooting for the other team and doesn't know it, but still, her kindness is unmistakable. I often ponder on the lavender I experienced in the Temple.

Justin is pure delight, loving and loveable, a gift that will help me endure the brutally difficult years ahead with him. The time before he starts school is the closest I will ever come to having a baby, a baby who is already walking and talking, but a baby who captures my heart with his every look, word, and move. He is a character, and I will never forget buckling him into his car seat after he's been naughty in the grocery store, about age three.

"When Mommy says no, the answer is no," would have been plenty, but I go on and on as I tend to do, and dead-pan, he looks up at me and delivers, "Blah blah blah" with perfect dismissiveness.

I love him more than life itself.

My mother, unexpectedly, is wonderful, everything a grandmother should be. She proudly displays a sign in her kitchen, "My grandchildren are the apple of my eye," and her face lights up in their presence. Sleepovers at Grandma's mean movies and popcorn, cookies fresh from the oven—an aroma that was not part of my childhood—and hot chocolate with sweet, sticky marshmallows. I've never seen her so happy, though still not with me. She notices my harshness with Kaylyn and points it out in her characteristically harsh way. The irony is rich, my harsh mother criticizing me for harshness to my daughter, and I lash out.

"You wouldn't last a week with this girl!"

I have long since denied my mother permission to guide me, but Kaylyn and her brothers bring a lot of healing to our relationship. The healing had started with Cary, the wonderful Cary Voss with his gorgeous blue eyes who I thought I was going to have to fight my mother for, his warm spirit softening us both. The gospel, the longer I live it, gives me more compassion and forgiveness, more peace with her. The realization that parenting is an impossible job heals our relationship most of all. Hard feelings I carry for things she's said and done over the years fade quickly in the face of my own horrible parenting moments.

The counselor teaches me a quartet of wisdom that I memorize: "All parents make mistakes. Lots of parents make lots of mistakes. A few parents make really terrible mistakes. Damage can be repaired in the way a parent handles mistakes."

I focus on taking responsibility and apologizing for my mistakes, something my mother never did, a thought I hold not as criticism of her but to underscore what apology from a parent means, what it would have meant to me.

For the last five years of her life, my mother and I become almost friends. With the kids between us, and with my new-found compassion and forgiveness, we find a way to interact that is lighter, more enjoyable. There is even, occasionally, easy laughter. When she dies of lung cancer, nine months after my father passes away from complications related to Alzheimer's, I won't realize for almost a week how devastated I am.

I've never needed my mother for anything, or so I think. It's true that I've never asked her for advice, and with the exception of the alcohol-fight-bite-police event, I've never called her when I was in trouble. But as a forty-four-year-old orphan, I encounter one of life's most profound truths: no one loves you like your mother. The anchor I didn't know I had is gone, the only one who really cared about my vacation photos, the only one who reveled as much as I do in my children's every breath.

The fear or grief or loneliness that kept us apart while she was living vanish, and I long for the woman who gave me life, who taught me to be a good person, who loved me to the end. She also, poignantly, showed me that good people can have colossal flaws and still be good people, a principle I will need to forgive myself one day.

She would be pleased to know, I believe she does know, that her death brings me and Kaylyn to the first mother-daughter sweetness we have had. In the startling discovery of how much my mother means to me, I let myself matter to my children. Whatever fear or grief or loneliness has kept me from being my real, vulnerable self with them vanishes, and I let them in.

My mother's memorial is a small affair, a few of us sitting around her living room telling stories about her. My favorite, told to me by my mother herself, is the time she threw food on the floor of a restaurant while on a date with my father. She had never liked that he was so reserved, was always trying to "get a rise out of him," as she put it.

I had responded incredulously, "And he married you anyway?"

She had lifted her regal chin and sniffed, "No, I married him anyway!"

I sit with my arms around Kaylyn and hers around me, leaning our heads together contentedly, listening to the rest of the stories. I am not normally physically affectionate with her, so this is unusual on its face; what is more unusual is the peace I feel, the absolute safety I feel loving her and letting her love me. It doesn't last, but it shows me a lighthouse, proof that safe harbor is there, a godsend because I am almost immediately lost at sea.

I take to my bed, watching TV, and eating bags and bags and bags of chocolate candy, sixty packed-on pounds worth before it is over. I get the kids off to school in the mornings, then go back to bed until they come home. I do only what I must to keep them safe, then go back to bed. My job is to keep them alive until Cary gets home from work, my sixty-year-old husband with a twelve-year-old, a nine-year-old, and a five-year-old. He makes dinner, does laundry, and helps with homework, managing all their difficult behaviors and treating me with tenderness and concern, a gesture I doubt I could reciprocate if our positions were reversed.

I rise from my bed six months later, changed by my mother's death into someone less tethered in the world, someone with nowhere to go for Christmas. My grief at her death releases me from the sharp edges of our relationship, allows me to love her unfettered, to feel close to her for the first time. I will think about her more often, understand her far better without the oil-and-water dynamic of our real life.

When Cary wakes up with an impression to move to Utah, I have nothing to keep me in San Diego, nothing but the fact that I am a California girl, through and through. California is a multidimensional universe, a place where anything is possible and everything exists, the perfect foil for my life.

Mormon Utah is another galaxy, a squeaky-clean—at least on the surface—wild, wild west, a cross between Texas—we make our own rules—and Mayberry—not a black person in sight. The population of the entire state—about three million—is that of San Diego County alone. I will make it work, but I will never fit in. The Mormon credo—"use it up, wear it out, make it do, or do without"—has never been my thing. Grocery stores don't carry alcohol, businesses close on Sundays, and "oh, my heck" peppers an atmosphere known as "the Mormon Bubble."

For our family, the move will be a fresh start, the beginning of what will become, finally, a real bond between us. For Cary, it will be the end of six-figure income; he will never recover the career he leaves behind. When my working outside the home would make it so much easier, he will humble himself and work an entry-level position at an hourly wage to support us. If it kills him, he's going to give me what I've longed for and what our particular kids can't thrive without—full-time motherhood. Of all the examples of manliness he ever shows, this will make me the proudest.

For me, the move is portended to spell the end of life as I know it. My Mormon friends in San Diego, all of whom have been raised in Utah, caution me that it's not possible for an outsider to make real friends.

"Nobody needs you," they inform me, "everybody's already best friends with their mother and sisters and cousins."

They are right about the juggernaut of family relationships, almost right that I will not be able to pierce it, but Heavenly Father has a plan for me, for our family.

My love of reading leads me to start a book club, which leads me to Chris, the youngest of ten, who spent time after high school as a nanny in New Jersey. The years away from her family showed her the jewel that nonfamily friendship can be, a jewel she continued to honor once back in Utah. She invites me into her tight-knit group: some devout Mormons, some not-so-devout, some inactive; a Baptist; a lapsed Catholic; a woman from Texas; and a lesbian couple, one of whom served a mission for the Church twenty years ago, one of whom floats on the verge of anti-Mormon. It is as eclectic as Northern Utah gets, and it is perfect for me, a critical first step in healing my broken parts.

Andy, the lesbian returned missionary tells me, "I don't know why I am the way I am, but the Church is true."

I see the pain in her eyes when she says it, the conflict between two loves, and I sense in her a kindred spirit, someone who also feels the wrenching divide between biblical Christianity and homosexuality. The connection moves me to come out of hiding, to be who I am, the first time I reveal all of myself to a group of people ever. They receive me with total acceptance, a powerful before and after. I will never go back. It will take more courage than I presently have, but I make the commitment to work toward a life where I never hide again.

My moment of wholeness is a reset, part vision, part facilitation of my best self. It does not, unfortunately, reset anything with the kids.

Utah is ideal for families: rope swings, bike paths, lakes, and children everywhere. Church is like Chuck E. Cheese with nicer clothes. We are led, of this I'm sure, to a particular neighborhood full of special needs kids, so many and so varied that my kids and their struggles are swallowed up in relative normalcy. Nearly every family is touched, nearly every child compassionate, nearly every parent understanding.

We have the gospel, we have the healing environment, and we also have every problem we've ever had plus a few new ones since the kids are getting older. Another universal of motherhood: the older they get, the less control I have. What I thought were intractable problems when they were younger are now not only intractable but exponentially more difficult. There is shoplifting, meetings with police, stealing caught on videotape, threatened suspensions, and still the screaming, always the screaming.

Justin, now eight, is out of control. A neuropsychologist cannot finish his testing, saying he's never seen anyone as hyperactive as Justin. Justin never sits down, never stops moving, never stops talking. He disrupts every meal, every family activity, every day at school. When he hears "no," he turns violent, destroying toys, tables, walls, and doors. We reluctantly try him on medication and make it worse.

It all catches up with me in Zumba class of all places, and I break down completely, crying so hard I have to leave the room. An older woman, a real-life guardian angel, follows me out and changes my life, changes all of our lives, by asking what's wrong.

"I'm sorry, I can't take it anymore!" I blubber. "I can't stand my kids, and they hate me! We adopted them, and they hate me! I don't know what to do!"

The next part of the plan unfolds.

The woman, whose name I never learn, leans in and says, "There's a woman I know who adopted four siblings. I'll give you her number. Maybe she can help."

She does help, this mother of four, throwing me cold, hard truth with a hope chaser.

"I hated my kids, too," she said. "I hated my life. My kids hated me. Then we found an attachment therapist."

Three weeks later, we drive an hour south to the same attachment therapist. Cary, Gavin, Kaylyn, and I sit in a row on Laura's couch. Justin bounces Legos at the little table in the corner. Young, blonde, and hip, Laura has presence. Her gentle eyes hold each one of us as she speaks.

I know we're in the right place when she says, "You're not crazy. I teach abnormal parenting."

Laura gives us all permission to hate each other, a shocking but freeing direction. I can feel the tension dissolve in our line, each of us collapsing as she says it, the truth that we have all lived for nearly eight years finally acknowledged.

She teaches us techniques—controversial in some quarters—to short-circuit the kids' fight-or-flight mode of reacting to us: jumping jacks, peanut butter sandwiches, and essays, brilliantly devised essays that encourage the kids to express their hate for us and, when that is no longer blocking everything else, the pain underneath.

I drive the hour south each week, sometimes two or three times, for more than a year. The kids, in fight-or-flight mode, can't flee so they fight us on everything, and things get much worse before they slowly, miraculously, get better. The pearl of great price, the catalyst for real transformation, is Laura's advice to me on anger.

"These attachment-disordered kids are very good at making parents angry. When they make you angry, they don't have to feel their own feelings. The only way they heal is if you stay positive."

It's embarrassing and petty, but as soon as I know my anger gives them what they want, I find a way to squelch it. It becomes a chess game, and we each take our turn. With Laura's coaching, instead of trying to stop Justin when he tantrums, I encourage him to yell louder, a foolproof method for killing a tantrum on the spot.

As the kids' behavior improves, my broken parts tick louder. There's a reason I'm invited to every therapy session with the kids: attachment is a family problem. Soon I am driving the hour south one more time each week, to meet with Laura by myself. I am brutally honest about my negative feelings and behavior toward Kaylyn.

"Thank you for your honesty, Donna. Usually when a parent struggles with a child like this, it's because she reminds you of someone. One of your parents maybe?"

I know Kaylyn is more like my mother than I am, but that doesn't feel like the source of my hostility. Working with Laura for months, praying for insight now rather than how to fix Kaylyn, I am stunned to realize that Kaylyn reminds me of me. Not the me I present to the world, not the me that survived my childhood, the me that I crushed in order to do it.

Kaylyn is soft, and sweet, and meek, a little giddy, and a lot flighty. I couldn't afford to be those things. I had to be a mini-adult, always on guard. I hate the weak, vulnerable parts of myself. I hate Kaylyn for being the things I hate about myself.

My inner thirteen-year-old with her stupid, weak needs is where she belongs, buried in a cement vault. Laura hangs in with me, using all of her skills, until I'm willing to consider forgiving myself for having needs, willing to try embracing that lonely little girl. Initially the idea makes me retch, my own fight-or-flight reaction to lowering my steel guard. Laura, doing what she is born to do, finds a way to soften the barricade, keeping me company as I bring it down.

In direct proportion to my softening, Kaylyn becomes more enjoyable for me to be around. As I enjoy her, she calms, and I enjoy her more. The only thing left, and I can't avoid it any longer, is to apologize to her, take responsibility for having been so cold for so long. I take her to the park with a couple of vanilla shakes. It's late fall, a warm afternoon though the air smells crisp, and we're in flip-flops and jeans. We watch the high school track team for a while; I'm too embarrassed to meet Kaylyn's eyes. Finally I do what I came to do.

"Kaylyn, this is hard for me to say. I know I've been really hard on you. A lot of times I've been mean."

I swallow hard. I don't know if I've already said the hardest part or if it's still ahead of me.

"If it weren't for you, I would never have known I had so much ugliness inside of me. I know it sounds weird, but I'm grateful to you for helping me find it so I could get rid of it. Can you forgive me and let me make it up to you?"

Kaylyn looks at me with tender, big brown eyes, rather remarkable since she struggles with empathy.

"It's okay, Mom, I forgive you. I love you."

"I love you, too," I smile. And I mean it.

Our moment in the park is both culmination and beginning. My life experience means nothing without this moment. It brings all that has gone before into purpose; the trauma, the adventure, the sorrow, the gospel. In what can be only divine orchestration, my lavender girl has called forth my healing so that I can call forth hers.

There is no magic, but we laugh more. When Gavin tells us at breakfast that he caught Kaylyn sleep-singing to her bunny, eyes closed, bunny stretched up over her face, we laugh until we cry. There are still mornings I don't want to come out of my room, and Cary's rare coin collection disappears when someone talks the babysitter into driving to the bank and trading it for thirteen one-dollar bills. But we're a family. We like each other, we annoy each other, we love each other, we keep each other company in the hurting places, we help each other grow.

Cary makes a sometimes fitful peace with his trials, emerging a finer, better, more faith-filled man. We accept that I am the one to take the kids skiing or hiking, but he plays a mean hand of hearts, which we love to do on Sundays, especially when it's snowing and we wear our pajamas. He handles everything soccer and never misses a game for any of the kids.

The kids adore him, and much to my only half-joking frustration—the one who is on the front lines all the time—always pick Cary as the subject of their school projects on heroes. He and Gavin go to car shows and talk about hunting and fishing. Kaylyn is her daddy's girl and couldn't have a better teddy bear to hug. She makes his lunch for work every night and writes little notes on the brown paper sack like "I love you" and "Have a great day" and "Thanks for being a great dad." Cary, standing carefully balanced in one spot, plays catch with Justin in the backyard. They have a special connection, and Justin does his homework—when he does it—in Cary's office so that he can be close to his hero.

When Gavin attains the rank of Eagle Scout—a tremendous accomplishment for any young man let alone one with Gavin's start in life—he gives me permission to share some of his journey with friends and family at the Court of Honor.

I talk about the raging fire when he sat down and waited to die, too frightened to wake his birth parents. I talk about him watching all the other kids eat their ice cream, too frightened to order his own. I talk about the day it changed, when he found the courage to knock on every door in the neighborhood because an elderly woman had lost her dog.

The privilege it is to be Gavin's mother wells up in me, and I sob, speaking more intensely as I share what dawns on me only now.

"If Gavin never graduates high school, if he never serves a mission, if he accomplishes nothing after this night, he is still a miracle!"

The tears shining back at me from around the room, even from men in the Eagles' Nest, Eagle Scouts all, tell me we all feel it, we all know what an incredible young man Gavin is to have reached the Eagles' Nest himself, despite everything. The intensity of the moment is broken when I demand, as only the mother of an Eagle Scout can, that he kiss my cheek for the picture. His embarrassed and laughing face and my proud and happy one are captured together in the photo, a sweet memory I gaze at often.

I hold my breath until Gavin graduates high school, even calling the office the day before commencement to make sure his name is on the diploma list. Gavin is smart, there's no doubt, but school is not his thing. After six years of my pushing and monitoring his school performance to no avail, Gavin resisting in every way possible, Laura gives us both some advice.

"Gavin, if you want to fail, we can't stop you. Mom, it's his choice. Let go, and see what he does."

The tension between us, source of thorny conflict for more than half a decade, disappears overnight. Later Gavin will tell me he never took his school responsibilities seriously because he knew I was his safety net, would catch and help him correct any problems. When I step back, he steps forward because he has to. We are all overjoyed to hear his name—Gavin Theodore Voss—called out as a graduating senior, an accomplishment no one can ever take away from him.

He buys a car—a 1999 Honda Accord—with money he's saved from a part-time job, endlessly tinkering with and improving the muffler—the louder the better, which makes me cringe—the stereo, the paint job, and every other aspect of his first love.

It is one of the deepest satisfactions of my life to see Gavin happy, working, saving money for school—Auto Tech unless he changes his mind—hanging out with his friends, dating a darling girl with her own college ambitions.

He's hardly ever home, and I tell him, "Go be nineteen. Enjoy your life."

It has been so long in coming. He deserves the chance to be carefree for once.

He may serve a mission, he may not. He may enlist in the army, he may not. He may go to school now, he may wait a year. What I know for sure is that he will be a loyal son and brother, a good citizen, a fiercely protective husband and father. I imagine the Sunday dinners we'll have with him throughout his journey, relishing each new phase together, so grateful, so proud to be his parents.

Kaylyn surprises me every day, the once-desperate duckling now a beautiful, self-confident swan. She expresses her feelings better than most of my peers, and better yet, isn't afraid to feel them anymore. She has the charming ability to laugh at herself, and she's quick to accept responsibility when she does wrong—something I never thought I would see.

I teach what I know—pick yourself up and brush yourself off—and Kaylyn may surpass the teacher. She moves through mistakes cleanly, not wanting to waste time on the past, and her maturity in self-correction is inspiring. Though a bit too chatty at times—something I hear at every parent-teacher conference—Kaylyn possesses the kind of substance, the kind of self-respect that attracts true friends.

The same neuropsychologist who said she hadn't had a need met since she came out of the birth canal also said she was at risk for oppositional defiant disorder. Cary and I can attest to that—nearly ten years of back talk and enough arguing to make me want to slit my wrists—yet today she is our easiest, most cheerful, most independent, most helpful, most thoughtful child. I love watching her unfold, her loveliness more apparent all the time.

Kaylyn's most magical quality, almost like fairy dust, is the effect she has on young girls, evident at family parties where she is always surrounded by half a dozen wide-eyed, adoring ones, each clamoring for her attention, hanging on her every word. They may not see her lavender, but they feel it.

She is seventeen and driving—a little scary—and just this side of her first boyfriend. It will be a while, but I can't wait to see what kind of mother she will be, can't wait to hold her babies in my arms, to feel a deepening of the connection we already share. Like Gavin, she is solid, someone I know I can count on.

Justin, my baby, the twelve-year-old love of my life, is a glorious work in progress, my magnum opus as a mother. He is still a Tigger, the life of the party, undecided on impulse control. When he throws his arms around me and says he loves me, it's worth everything. His kiss on my cheek makes my heart flutter. His relentless obsession with Minecraft makes my eye twitch. Charismatic and manipulative, he will be, I encourage him, the greatest of salesmen. Or entrepreneurs. How he gets kids to pay actual dollars for his Minecraft Papercraft figures, painstakingly cut out and glued in every spare minute—and when he's supposed to be sleeping or doing his chores—is a mystery, but that's why I see his name up in lights.

A love of work he does not have. The three years of teaching it takes before he makes his bed independently—and quasi-neatly—are a tribute to my perseverance. Watching him make it without attitude is better than the corner office and stock options.

Justin is not fond of rules, has never met one, in fact, that he likes. The Lord knew that for Justin to thrive, he would need the gospel, Laura, a mother who never gives up, the examples of Gavin and Kaylyn, and a father—Cary—who makes it all possible. The Lord knew our family would need Justin, the most special of spirits, to hold us together until we could bond.

Justin is watched over by angels; we feel them around us. When Cary and I decided to pray for the children headed to our home, we had no way of knowing that Justin's birth mother, pregnant with him at the time, had rolled a truck, and doctors said the baby might not live. I didn't know why he needed our prayers, but something inspired me to reach toward him, a connection that may have saved both of our lives.

Cary and I have roller-coastered through twelve years of marriage, the worst and now best years of my life. What we each lacked in vision—both of us attempting to stop our relationship before it started—we made up for in dedication to the Lord's vision. If either of us had faltered, and we were sorely tempted many times, we would have missed the joy he was guiding us toward, most of which springs from the deep bond we ourselves have forged. For two people with almost nothing in common, I couldn't love Cary more.

When we muse from time to time about life after the kids are grown, I see Sunday dinners, gourmet meals that I lovingly prepare for an ever-growing posterity. I see holidays and summer barbecues, family reunions, and vacations. I see making my children's spouses feel welcome, teaching my grandchildren to cook, to ski, to love learning. Cary sees, he tells me with a wicked grin, NASCAR. He has always dreamed of traveling the country during the season, visiting each racetrack in turn. I suppose if I can handle Gavin, Kaylyn, and Justin, I can handle anything.

I don't see the sharp detail of active Mormon Church membership for us all. It's not that I see its absence, I simply don't know, and although I have a clear preference, I really don't care all that much. Maybe I should, but caring too much is the opposite to me of accepting my children for who they are, of honoring their agency the way Gregg honored mine. If Gregg had communicated to me that I was less than, or needed to become a Mormon to be better, I wouldn't be here today. It was only because of his total acceptance—total—that my heart opened to what mattered to him. I can't think of a better model for loving, and accepting, my children.

My children know I love the gospel and why. I've taught them gospel principles to the best of my ability, and I've raised them with Mormon values, the best, to my view, values there are. What they choose to do with it all, how they go forward, is up to them. It is the privilege of a human life—given to us by God himself—to choose for ourselves what to believe and how to live.

It is even codified in our article of faith: "We claim the privilege of worshiping Almighty God according to the dictates of our own conscience, and allow all men the same privilege, let them worship how, where, or what they may."

That's the doctrine I believe in, that's the church I belong to.

Our family has found its groove, and it's sweet. When we entertain, which we do often, there's a delight in being together, welcoming family and friends to our home. We host the family for Thanksgiving and try to invite new families in the neighborhood for dinner. In summer, Cary grills, and I make deviled eggs and lemon squares. We set a sprinkler under the trampoline for the little girls, to whom Kaylyn is the most beautiful princess they've ever seen. Justin hosts the rough-and-tumble boys at Foosball and air hockey. Gavin brings his cute girlfriend for burgers and dogs. The only fireworks now are on the Fourth of July, ones we watch as a family from the fifty-yard line at the high school.

I wouldn't change a thing in my past because I wouldn't trade where it led me. I love where I am today, trust that the experiences I've had were the right ones for me. Every difficult moment I've had makes me appreciate the sweet ones.

I'm grateful to my parents, two of the best people I've ever known, for the foundation they gave me in life. I'm grateful to Gregg for being a true friend and teaching me who I really am, where I come from, where I'm going. I'm grateful to Andy for demonstrating grace in the face of unbridgeable loyalties. I'm grateful to Laura for defining the problem correctly and for giving us the tools to solve it.

I'm grateful to Cary for seeing beyond my past and for making our family possible. His willingness to sacrifice so much to give me motherhood is its own inestimable gift.

I'm grateful to my children for calling forth my best self and for honoring me with their trust. Because of them, I have tasted Christlike love.

I'm grateful to feel whole, not afraid anymore to own who I am.

All things work together for good to them that love God.

AFTERWORD

"To see that your life is a story while you're in the middle of living it may be a help to living it well."
—URSULA K. LE GUIN
Gifts

O nce a mother, always a mother; that is the core of who I am and will be forever. Although the sun isn't quite setting on full-time motherhood, it's starting to dip in the sky, and new challenges call to me. I could happily go back to a career in health care, or use my MBA for something else, but my new dream is writing.

As a lark, I went to a writer's conference, no pressure, no expectations. I had no idea that everyone brings writing samples to these conferences, and all I had with me on my laptop was something I'd written for fun, a soliloquy of sorts on being a Berkeley grad with a cosmopolitan life behind me now living in rural, white-bread Utah.

Beginner's luck brought me to the attention of an intrigued agent, who promptly requested and then rejected three complete chapters when my expanded, made-to-order writing lacked voice, whatever that meant. But she gave me the idea.

I wrote a complete draft of my story with what I thought was more voice and pretty good writing. Fifty query letters to fifty agents later, none of whom responded positively, few of whom responded at all, I almost gave up. It turned out to be the best thing that could have happened.

What I learned the hard, valuable way is that writing is like pregnancy: relatively easy to get started—all fun and excitement at the beginning—extremely challenging to gestate and deliver the baby.

I went to more writers' conferences, refined my focus, and started over from scratch, writing three to four hours a night when everyone else was asleep. I wrote and rewrote until I found my voice, hammered out my creative process, mastered some techniques, and felt the baby kick. Eventually as much thrill as effort, I practiced painting with words, sculpting a story, and evoking emotion. It became deeply satisfying, as fulfilling as I imagine any pregnancy could be.

Like pregnancy, I couldn't do it without a man—Cary— who makes writing, like he makes everything else, possible for me. It is no small investment of time, energy, and resources to write and publish a book, yet Cary holds no encouragement back. At sixty-seven, he is more than ready to retire but continues to work full time for our family, for me, so that I can explore this dream of telling my story, of telling all kinds of future stories.

Because it is not my story alone, I read aloud to my children every word that I wrote about them, giving them carte blanche to add, edit, or delete anything they wished. They changed nothing; in fact, they clapped when I finished. The experience of sharing our story out loud brought us closer.

I still think of Job, the faithful man who lost everything, or thought he did, and whose end was made better than his beginning by an even more faithful God. What I thought I had lost in not bearing children, the Lord has more than made up to me. I'm grateful I didn't bear children, because I would not be mother to Gavin, Kaylyn, and Justin if I had.

There are all kinds of creations, all kinds of births. I have the children I was meant to have, and my book is ready to be born. The Lord's vision for me has always been grander than anything I can envision for myself.

I can't wait to see what happens next.

ACKNOWLEDGEMENTS

Words are inadequate to acknowledge Gregg Prettyman for his friendship that changed my life, changed me, and showed me the eternal vision of who I am.

Words are woefully inadequate to acknowledge Cary Voss for his love in action: his willingness to sacrifice so much for me to be mother to my most important teachers; his steady commitment to our family through thick and thin; his unfailing belief in me; and his generous enthusiasm for this project.

My parents did the best they could with what they had; they were such good people, and I owe them my integrity, my manners, and my compassion.

This book would never have come to be without Antoinette Kuritz and The La Jolla Writer's Conference of which she is the founder.

As tends to happen in life, seemingly random events brought the three of us together in November of 2011. Seated on large white Adirondack chairs between workshops, Antoinette and I began what would turn out to be both working relationship and deep friendship, although it is much more than both.

When I was ready to shelve the whole project out of frustration, Antoinette gave me the vision of what it could be. The first line of the book flows directly from our conversation that afternoon.

She encouraged me, mentored me, laughed with me, and challenged me. She brought me to the dance, introducing me to some very fine people, all of whom contributed to the book you hold in your hands.

Writing such a deeply personal book requires not a small amount of courage, and I would never have taken the risk without absolute trust in Antoinette's instincts, expertise, and sincerity.

She is a rock star!